POWER

— T O —

BECOME

P O W E R

— T O —

BECOME

Spiritual patterns for pressing forward
with a steadfastness in Christ

DAVID A. BEDNAR

DESERET
BOOK

SALT LAKE CITY, UTAH

Library of Congress Cataloging-in-Publication Data
Bednar, David A., author.
  Power to become / David A. Bednar.
      pages cm
  Includes bibliographical references and index.
  ISBN 978-1-60907-859-1 (hardbound : alk. paper)
  1. Christian life—Mormon authors. 2. The Church of Jesus Christ of Latter-day Saints—
Doctrines. 3. Mormon Church—Doctrines. I. Title.
  BX8656.B4395 2014
  248.4'89332—dc23   2013042047

Printed in the United States of America
Publishers Printing, Salt Lake City, UT

10   9   8   7   6   5   4

To family members, friends, and
faithful Latter-day Saints all over
the world in whom I have seen
and from whom I have learned
about the power to become

Contents

ACKNOWLEDGMENTS

I am thankful to my wife, Susan, for her love, her encouragement, and her steadfast example of the power to become. I also express appreciation to Shauna Swainston for her timely assistance and support; and to Sheri Dew for her thoughtful suggestions and input.

The publishing team at Deseret Book has worked with professionalism and excellence. Thanks go to Laurel Christensen Day for overseeing the project; Emily Watts for her expert counsel, editing, and assistance in preparing the manuscript for publication; Richard Erickson and Sheryl Dickert Smith for the design; Rachael Ward for the typography; and Elizabeth Alley for her help with the online teaching segments. Heartfelt thanks to our family, friends, and associates who have been so instrumental in helping me formulate and refine the ideas presented in this book. I am grateful for all of the individuals, both named and unnamed, who have inspired, supported, and assisted me in writing *Power to Become*.

This book is not an official statement of Church doctrine, policy, or practice, and I alone am responsible for the content of *Power to Become*.

PREFACE

The title for this book comes from a passage in the Doctrine and Covenants:

"Behold, I am Jesus Christ, the Son of God. I am the life and the light of the world.

"I am the same who came unto mine own and mine own received me not;

"But verily, verily, I say unto you, that as many as receive me, to them will I give *power to become* the sons [and daughters] of God, even to them that believe on my name. Amen" (Doctrine and Covenants 11:28–30; emphasis added; see also Doctrine and Covenants 39:4; 42:52; John 1:12).

This volume builds upon and extends the spiritual patterns described in *Increase in Learning* and *Act in Doctrine* and discusses how we can be blessed to receive the "power to become."

Moroni is one of my spiritual heroes. The son of Mormon, the abridger of the book of Ether, and the final writer in the Book of Mormon, Moroni played a significant role in the Restoration of the gospel of Jesus Christ in the latter days. As I have studied the life and ministry of this mighty prophet, I have returned again and again to a specific verse in the Book of Mormon that I believe reveals a great deal about his spiritual devotion, depth, and experience.

In the tenth and final chapter of the book of Moroni, he declares that a testimony of the Book of Mormon comes by the power of the Holy Ghost, that spiritual gifts are dispensed to the faithful, and that we are to come unto Christ and be perfected in Him. As he then concludes his record, he says good-bye to his future readers and proclaims his final witness and testimony.

"And now I bid unto all, farewell. I soon go to rest in the paradise of God, until my spirit and body shall again reunite, and I am brought forth triumphant through the air, to meet you before the pleasing bar of the great Jehovah, the Eternal Judge of both quick and dead. Amen" (Moroni 10:34).

The phrase I find most interesting in this verse is "the *pleasing* bar of the great Jehovah, the Eternal Judge of both quick and dead" (emphasis added). Please note that Moroni described the judgment bar of the great Jehovah as *pleasing*. Many individuals likely find the thought of standing before the Eternal Judge to be frightening, intimidating, overwhelming, tormenting, and daunting—many things other than pleasing. But Moroni was not fearful of or apprehensive about this inevitable day of reckoning. He looked forward to meeting us at the *pleasing* bar of the great Jehovah! Moroni understood before his death, at least in part, what awaited him beyond the veil.

A simple question arises in my mind and heart from this benedictory scripture: How could and did Moroni come to know in mortality that the judgment bar of the great Jehovah would be pleasing?

Can you and I, like Moroni, truly come to know that the path we are pursuing in our lives pleases God? And if it is possible to know these things, how can we know? Such questions indeed are some of the most pointed and poignant questions of the soul.

As we increase in learning about the Savior and His gospel, as we strive with ever greater consistency to act in His doctrine, ordinances, and covenants, then we are blessed with power through His Atonement to increasingly become like Him. Our hearts and natures are changed, and our desires are directed to Him and His purposes. His will supersedes our will. His desires supplant our desires. His purposes become our purposes. These changes rarely occur quickly, dramatically, or all at once; rather, they come into our lives "line upon line, precept upon precept, here a little and there a little" (2 Nephi 28:30).

But how can we really know how we are doing, and if our course is in accordance with God's will? In *Power to Become*, I attempt to present gospel truths, principles, and patterns that can help each of us as we strive to press forward with steadfastness and find for ourselves the answers to these eternally essential questions.

Power to Become is formatted with extra-wide margins for recording thoughts, impressions, and questions. It is meant to be an interactive experience—not just a book to read but a springboard for your own process of learning. Each chapter ends with a few questions that I hope you will consider, along with space to record your own questions and the answers you are receiving. An invitation to learn and act upon the principles discussed in the chapter is also included, with three interrelated questions that should be considered together but responded to individually. Thus, all three questions are repeated at the top of each response page, and the one to be addressed specifically on that page is highlighted.

Each chapter also includes a QR code, along with a printed

URL. These link to short videos of personal discussions I have con-
ducted with various groups on the topics in the chapters.

My hope is that this book will cause you to ponder, pray, reflect, evaluate, act, and progress spiritually. May the combination
of your faith in the Savior, your willingness to act as an agent, the
text, and the learning experiences in which you will engage invite
the Holy Ghost to help you more fully understand basic gospel
truths and spiritual patterns—to the end that each of us may be
blessed to receive the **POWER TO BECOME**.

CHAPTER 1

POWER TO BECOME AND THE
ATONEMENT OF JESUS CHRIST

As we honor sacred covenants, obey God's commandments, seek for the companionship of the Holy Ghost, and fulfill faithfully our personal responsibilities to "increase in learning" (Proverbs 9:9) and "act in doctrine" (Doctrine and Covenants 101:78), we can be blessed with the "power to become."

"Behold, I am Jesus Christ, the Son of God. I am the life and the light of the world.

"I am the same who came unto mine own and mine own received me not;

"But verily, verily, I say unto you, that as many as receive me, to them will I give *power to become* the sons [and daughters] of God, even to them that believe on my name. Amen" (Doctrine and Covenants 11:28–30; emphasis added; see also Doctrine and Covenants 39:4; 42:52; John 1:12).

The primary purposes of devoted discipleship are to "awaken" unto God (Alma 5:7; 7:22), to be "born again" (John 3:3; Mosiah 27:25; Alma 5:49; 7:14), to put off the natural man (see Mosiah 3:19), and to become "new" in Christ. "Therefore if any man be in

1

Christ, he is a new creature: old things are passed away; behold, all things are become new" (2 Corinthians 5:17). We also are to "press forward with a steadfastness in Christ" (2 Nephi 31:20) and endure in faith on His name to the end (see Matthew 24:13; 2 Nephi 31:16; Doctrine and Covenants 14:7; 20:29).

Ultimately, followers of Christ are to become like Him.

"Yea, come unto Christ, and be perfected in him, and deny yourselves of all ungodliness; and if ye shall deny yourselves of all ungodliness, and love God with all your might, mind and strength, then is his grace sufficient for you, that by his grace ye may be perfect in Christ; and if by the grace of God ye are perfect in Christ, ye can in nowise deny the power of God.

"And again, if ye by the grace of God are perfect in Christ, and deny not his power, then are ye sanctified in Christ by the grace of God, through the shedding of the blood of Christ, which is in the covenant of the Father unto the remission of your sins, that ye become holy, without spot" (Moroni 10:32–33).

"But charity is the pure love of Christ, and it endureth forever; and whoso is found possessed of it at the last day, it shall be well with him.

"Wherefore, my beloved brethren, pray unto the Father with all the energy of heart, that ye may be filled with this love, which he hath bestowed upon all who are true followers of his Son, Jesus Christ; that ye may become the sons of God; that when he shall appear we shall be like him, for we shall see him as he is; that we may have this hope; that we may be purified even as he is pure. Amen" (Moroni 7:47–48; see also 1 John 3:2).

Elder Dallin H. Oaks explained the importance of emulating and striving to become like the Savior:

"The Apostle Paul taught that the Lord's teachings and teachers were given that we may all attain 'the measure of the stature of the fulness of Christ' (Eph. 4:13). This process requires far more than acquiring knowledge. It is not even enough for us to be *convinced* of the gospel; we must act and think so that we are *converted* by it. In contrast to the institutions of the world, which teach us to *know* something, the gospel of Jesus Christ challenges us to *become* something.

"Many Bible and modern scriptures speak of a final judgment at which all persons will be rewarded according to their deeds or works or the desires of their hearts. But other scriptures enlarge upon this by referring to our being judged by the *condition* we have achieved.

"The prophet Nephi describes the Final Judgment in terms of what we *have become:* 'And if their works have been filthiness they must needs *be* filthy; and if they *be* filthy it must needs be that they cannot dwell in the kingdom of God' (1 Ne. 15:33; emphasis added). Moroni declares, 'He that *is* filthy shall be filthy still; and he that *is* righteous shall be righteous still' (Morm. 9:14; emphasis added; see also Rev. 22:11–12; 2 Ne. 9:16; D&C 88:35). The same would be true of 'selfish' or 'disobedient' or any other personal attribute inconsistent with the requirements of God. Referring to the 'state' of the wicked in the Final Judgment, Alma explains that if we are condemned by our words, our works, and our thoughts, 'we shall not be found spotless; . . . and in this awful state we shall not dare to look up to our God' (Alma 12:14).

"From such teachings we conclude that the Final Judgment is not just an evaluation of a sum total of good and evil acts—what we have *done.* It is an acknowledgment of the final effect of our acts and thoughts—what we have *become.* It is not enough for anyone just to go through the motions. The commandments, ordinances, and covenants of the gospel are not a list of deposits required to be made in some heavenly account. The gospel of Jesus Christ is a plan that shows us how to become what our Heavenly Father desires us to become" ("The Challenge to Become," 32; emphasis in original).

Righteous learning and acting can lead to "becoming" only by and through and because of the Savior's Atonement. The word *become* denotes growing, developing, changing, transforming, and converting. As we "come unto Christ" and seek perfection in and through Him (see Moroni 10:32–33), we incrementally and increasingly obtain His mind (see Philippians 2:5) and character. We put off the natural man and are fundamentally changed, transformed, and "converted unto the Lord" (Alma 23:6). The gospel and the Atonement of Jesus Christ fundamentally are about change—about helping us as sons and daughters of God to progress in becoming more like Him. Heavenly Father's plan of happiness establishes the framework for eternal progression, and the Savior's gospel provides the doctrines, covenants, and ordinances necessary to become what children of God are intended to become.

The depth and intensity of the Father's love for each of His children is evidenced in His willingness to allow His Only Begotten Son to offer the infinite and eternal atoning sacrifice (see Alma 34:10, 14). And it is the Atonement that enables us to learn, to act, to grow, and to receive the power to become like our Heavenly Father and His Beloved Son.

> *How great the wisdom and the love*
> *That filled the courts on high*
> *And sent the Savior from above*
> *To suffer, bleed, and die!*

His precious blood he freely spilt;
His life he freely gave,
A sinless sacrifice for guilt,
A dying world to save.

By strict obedience Jesus won
The prize with glory rife:
"Thy will, O God, not mine be done,"
Adorned his mortal life.

He marked the path and led the way,
And ev'ry point defines
To light and life and endless day
Where God's full presence shines.
("How Great the Wisdom and the Love,"
Hymns, *no. 195)*

"Be Ye Therefore Perfect"

If we are to become what Heavenly Father yearns for us to become, then what is the ultimate objective of our becoming?

In the holy scriptures the Lord provides the answer to this eternally important question.

"Be ye therefore perfect, even as your Father which is in heaven is perfect" (Matthew 5:48).

"Therefore I would that ye should be perfect even as I, or your Father who is in heaven is perfect" (3 Nephi 12:48).

"Therefore, what manner of men ought ye to be? Verily I say unto you, even as I am" (3 Nephi 27:27).

Latter-day prophets and apostles frequently have taught about our responsibility to press forward on the pathway of perfection. Please note the common themes in the messages of these inspired leaders.

"We consider that God has created man with a mind capable of instruction, and a faculty which may be enlarged in proportion to the heed and diligence given to the light communicated from heaven to the intellect; and that the nearer man approaches perfection, the clearer are his views, and the greater his enjoyments, till he has overcome the evils of his life and lost every desire for sin; and like the ancients, arrives at that point of faith where he is wrapped in the power and glory of his Maker, and is caught up to dwell with Him" (Joseph Smith, *History of the Church,* 2:8).

"When you climb up a ladder, you must begin at the bottom, and ascend step by step, until you arrive at the top; and so it is with the principles of the gospel—you must begin with the first, and go on until you learn all the principles of exaltation. But it will be a great while after you have passed through the veil before you will have learned them" (*Teachings of Presidents of the Church: Joseph Smith,* 268).

"It may appear strange to some of you, and it certainly does to the world, to say it is possible for a man or woman to become perfect on this earth. It is written, 'Be ye therefore perfect, even as your Father which is in heaven is perfect.' Again, 'If any man offend not in word, the same is a perfect man, and able also to bridle the whole body.' This is perfectly consistent to the person who understands what perfection really is.

"If the first passage I have quoted is not worded to our understanding we can alter the phraseology of the sentence, and say, 'Be ye as perfect as ye can,' for that is all we can do, though it is written, be ye perfect as your Father who is in heaven is perfect. . . . When we are doing as well as we know how in the sphere and station which we occupy here, we are justified in the justice, righteousness, mercy, and judgment that go before the Lord of heaven and earth. We are as justified as the angels who are before the throne of God. The sin that will cleave to all the posterity of Adam and Eve is, that they have not done as well as they knew how.

"When we use the term perfection, it applies to man in his present condition, as well as to heavenly beings. We are now, or may be, as perfect in our sphere as God and angels are in theirs, but the greatest intelligence in existence can continually ascend to greater heights of perfection" (*Discourses of Brigham Young*, 89).

"I believe the Lord meant just what he said: that we should be perfect, as our Father in heaven is perfect. That will not come all at once, but line upon line, and precept upon precept, example upon example, and even then not as long as we live in this mortal life, for we will have to go even beyond the grave before we reach that perfection. . . .

"But here we lay the foundation. Here is where we are taught these simple truths of the gospel of Jesus Christ, in this probationary state, to prepare us for that perfection. It is our duty to be better today than we were yesterday, and better tomorrow than we are today. Why? Because . . . if we are keeping the commandments of the Lord, we are on that road to perfection, and that can only come through obedience and the desire in our hearts to overcome the world.

"It is the duty of every man to try to be like his Eternal Father" (Joseph Fielding Smith, *Doctrines of Salvation*, 2:18–19).

"Would you suppose the Savior was suggesting a goal that was not possible of attainment and thus mock us in our efforts to live to attain that perfectness? It is impossible for us here in mortality to come to that state of perfection of which the Master spoke, but in this life we lay the foundation on which we will build in eternity; therefore, we must make sure that our foundation is laid on truth, righteousness, and faith. In order for us to reach that goal we must keep God's commandments and be true to the end of our lives here, and then beyond the grave continue in righteousness and knowledge until we become as our Father in Heaven. In wonderful revelations the Lord has told us that those 'who overcome by faith and are sealed by the Holy Spirit of Promise which the Father sheds forth upon all those who are just and true . . . they are they who are the Church of the Firstborn . . . into whose hands the Father hath given all things. They are they who are priests and kings who have received of his fulness and of his glory' (D. & C. 76:53–56). 'Every person who has this hope in him, purifieth himself even as God is pure' (1 John 3:3).

"Apparently the Apostle Paul thought this was a true doctrine for we find him declaring to members of the Church in his day: 'Let this mind be in you, which was also in Christ Jesus: Who, being in the form of God, thought it not robbery to be equal with God' (Philippians 2:5–6). He furthermore pointed to the course by which perfection comes. Speaking of Jesus, he said, 'Though he were a Son, yet learned he obedience by the things which he suffered; and being made perfect, he became the author of eternal salvation unto all them that obey him' (Hebrews 5:8–9)" (Harold B. Lee, *Decisions for Successful Living*, 40–41).

"And how to work toward perfection in our lives? It is not a one-time decision to be made, but a process to be pursued, slowly and laboriously through a lifetime. We build from simple building blocks, adding refinements as the building rises towards the heavens" (*The Teachings of Spencer W. Kimball,* 166).

"A man can ask no more important question in his life than that which Paul asked: 'Lord, what wilt thou have me to do?' [Acts 9:6.] A man can take no greater action than to pursue a course that will bring to him the answer to that question and then to carry out that answer. What would the Lord Jesus Christ have us do? He answered that question by saying, 'Be ye therefore perfect, even as your Father which is in heaven is perfect' (Matthew 5:48), and, 'Therefore, what manner of men ought ye to be? Verily, I say unto you, even as I am' (3 Nephi 27:27).

"Christ, then, has set us the example of what we should be like and what we should do. . . . This Jesus is our exemplar and has commanded us to follow in His steps" (Ezra Taft Benson, *God, Family, Country,* 155–56).

"In this life, certain actions can be perfected. A baseball pitcher can throw a no-hit, no-run ball game. A surgeon can perform an operation without an error. A musician can render a selection without a mistake. One can likewise achieve perfection in being punctual, paying tithing, keeping the Word of Wisdom, and so on. The enormous effort required to attain such self-mastery is rewarded with a deep sense of satisfaction. More importantly, spiritual attainments in mortality accompany us into eternity. . . .

"Mortal perfection can be achieved as we try to perform every duty, keep every law, and strive to be as perfect in our sphere as our Heavenly Father is in his. If we do the best we can, the Lord will bless us according to our deeds and the desires of our hearts.

"But Jesus asked for more than mortal perfection. The moment he uttered the words 'even as your Father which is in heaven is perfect,' he raised our sights beyond the bounds of mortality. Our Heavenly Father has eternal perfection. This very fact merits a much broader perspective.

"Recently I studied the English and Greek editions of the New Testament, concentrating on each use of the term *perfect* and its derivatives. Studying both languages together provided some interesting insights, since Greek was the original language of the New Testament.

"In Matthew 5:48, the term *perfect* was translated from the Greek *teleios,* which means 'complete.' *Teleios* is an adjective derived from the noun *telos,* which means 'end.' The infinitive form of the verb is *teleiono,* which means 'to reach a distant end, to be fully developed, to consummate, or to finish.' Please note that the word does not imply 'freedom from error'; it implies 'achieving a distant objective.' In fact, when writers of the Greek New Testament wished to describe perfection of behavior—precision or excellence of human effort—they did *not* employ a form of *teleios;* instead, they chose different words.

"*Teleios* is not a total stranger to us. From it comes the prefix *tele-* that we use every day. *Telephone* literally means 'distant talk.' *Television* means 'to see distantly.' *Telephoto* means 'distant light,' and so on.

"With that background in mind, let us consider another highly significant statement made by the Lord. Just prior to his crucifixion, he said that on 'the third day *I shall be perfected.*' Think of that! The sinless, errorless Lord—already perfect by our mortal standards—proclaimed his own state of perfection yet to be in the future. His *eternal* perfection would follow his resurrection and receipt of 'all power . . . in heaven and in earth.'

"The perfection that the Savior envisions for us is much more than errorless performance. It is the eternal expectation as expressed by the Lord in his great intercessory prayer to his Father—that we might be made perfect and be able to dwell with them in the eternities ahead" (Russell M. Nelson, "Perfection Pending," 86–87; emphasis in original).

THE CHARACTER OF CHRIST

What is the nature or type of perfection for which we are striving? The very character of Jesus provides the answer to this question.

One of the greatest indicators of righteous character is the capacity to recognize and appropriately respond to other people who are experiencing the very challenge or adversity that is most immediately and forcefully pressing upon us. Character is revealed, for example, in the power to discern the suffering of other people when we ourselves are suffering; in the ability to detect the hunger of others when we are hungry; and in the power to reach out and extend compassion for the spiritual agony of others when we are in the midst of our own spiritual distress. Thus, character is demonstrated by looking, turning, and reaching outward when the instinctive response of the "natural man" (Mosiah 3:19) is to turn inward and to be selfish and self-absorbed.

The Savior always turned outward in compassion and service—especially as He faced spiritual adversity and physical pain. The Master's capacity to bless and minister to others in the midst of His own affliction "marked the path and led the way" ("How Great the Wisdom and the Love," *Hymns,* no. 195) whereby during our mortal probation, through the power and efficacy of His Atonement, we can put off the selfish tendencies of the natural man and act more consistently in true doctrine.

Jesus Christ was sinless and divinely selfless; He is the source, the standard, and the ultimate criterion of moral character and the perfect example of charity and consistency.

Grace to Grace

The absolute enormity of perfection as an eternal goal or outcome may cause us to feel helplessly overwhelmed, inadequate, and discouraged. But as we learn from the teachings of the Brethren earlier in this chapter, perfection is not achieved all at once or in mortality. Even our perfect example, the Savior, progressed "line upon line, precept upon precept" (2 Nephi 28:30).

"And I, John, bear record that I beheld his glory, as the glory of the Only Begotten of the Father, full of grace and truth, even the Spirit of truth, which came and dwelt in the flesh, and dwelt among us.

"And I, John, saw that he received not of the fulness at the first, but received grace for grace;

"And he received not of the fulness at first, but continued from grace to grace, until he received a fulness;

"And thus he was called the Son of God, because he received not of the fulness at the first" (Doctrine and Covenants 93:11–14).

And the same pattern that applied to the Redeemer also applies to us.

"I give unto you these sayings that you may understand and know how to worship, and know what you worship, that you may come unto the Father in my name, and in due time receive of his fulness.

"For if you keep my commandments you shall receive of his fulness, and be glorified in me as I am in the Father; therefore, I say unto you, you shall receive grace for grace" (Doctrine and Covenants 93:19–20).

We also do not pursue perfection alone or rely exclusively upon the puny possibilities of the natural man or woman in each of us. We can depend upon help, strength, and support from heaven. The Savior declared: "If ye love me, keep my commandments.

"And I will pray the Father, and he shall give you another Comforter, that he may abide with you for ever;

"Even the Spirit of truth; whom the world cannot receive, because it seeth him not, neither knoweth him: but ye know him; for he dwelleth with you, and shall be in you.

"*I will not leave you comfortless:* I will come to you" (John 14:15–18; emphasis added).

> *Fear not, I am with thee; oh, be not dismayed,*
> *For I am thy God and will still give thee aid.*
> *I'll strengthen thee, help thee, and cause thee to stand,*
> *Upheld by my righteous, omnipotent hand.*
> *("How Firm a Foundation," Hymns, no. 85)*

IN THE STRENGTH OF THE LORD

For disciples of Jesus Christ, the journey of mortality proceeds along the pathway to perfection. The Savior's Atonement strengthens and enables us to press forward with steadfastness and perseverance. Our limited mortal capacity can be enlarged to meet the requirements of the divine injunction—"Be ye therefore perfect" (Matthew 5:48).

The grand objective of the Savior's gospel was summarized succinctly by President David O. McKay, as quoted by Elder Franklin D. Richards: "The purpose of the gospel is . . . to make bad men good and good men better, and to change human nature" (in Conference Report, October 1965, 136–37). Thus, the journey of mortality is to progress from bad to good to better and to experience the mighty change of heart—to have our fallen natures changed (see Mosiah 5:2) and to be "perfected in Him" (Moroni 10:32–33).

The Book of Mormon is a handbook of instructions as we travel the trail from bad to good to better and strive to have our hearts changed. King Benjamin teaches about the journey of mortality and the role of the Atonement in successfully navigating that journey: "For the natural man is an enemy to God, and has been from the fall of Adam, and will be, forever and ever, unless he yields to the enticings of the Holy Spirit, *and putteth off the natural man and becometh a saint* through the atonement of Christ the Lord" (Mosiah 3:19; emphasis added).

I draw your attention to two specific phrases. First—"putteth off the natural man." The journey from bad to good is the process of putting off the natural man or the natural woman in each of us. In mortality we all are tempted by the flesh. The very elements out of which our bodies were created are by nature fallen and ever subject to the pull of sin, corruption, and death. But we can increase our capacity to overcome the desires of the flesh and temptations "through the atonement of Christ." When we make mistakes, as we transgress and sin, we can repent and become clean through the redeeming power of the Atonement of Jesus Christ.

Second—"becometh a saint." This phrase describes the continuation and second phase of life's journey to make "good men better," or, in other words, to become more like a saint. This second part of the journey, this process of going from good to better, is a topic about which we do not study or teach frequently enough. I believe we do not understand it adequately.

I suspect that many Church members are much more familiar with the nature of the redeeming and cleansing power of the Atonement of Jesus Christ than they are with the strengthening and enabling power. It is one thing to know that Jesus Christ came to earth to *die* for us—that is fundamental and foundational to the doctrine of Christ. But we also need to appreciate that the Lord desires, through His Atonement and by the power of the Holy Ghost, to *live* in us—not only to direct us but also to empower us.

Most of us know that when we do wrong things, we need help to overcome the effects of sin in our lives. The Savior has paid the price and made it possible for us to become clean through His redeeming power. Most of us clearly understand that the Atonement is for sinners.

I am not so sure, however, that we know and understand that the Atonement is also for saints—for good men and women who are obedient, worthy, and conscientious and who are striving to become better and serve more faithfully. We may mistakenly believe we must make the journey from good to better and become saints all by ourselves, through sheer grit, willpower, and discipline, and with our obviously limited capacities.

The gospel of the Savior is not simply about avoiding bad in our lives; it also is essentially about doing and becoming good. And the Atonement provides help for us to overcome and avoid bad as well as to do and become good. Help from the Savior is available for the entire journey of mortality—from bad to good to better—and to change our very nature.

I am not suggesting that the redeeming and enabling powers of the Atonement are separate and discrete. Rather, these two dimensions of the Atonement are connected and complementary; they both need to be operational during all phases of the journey of life. And it is eternally important for all of us to recognize that *both* of these essential elements of the journey of mortality—both putting off the natural man and becoming a saint, both overcoming bad and becoming good—are accomplished through the power of the

Savior's Atonement. Individual willpower, personal determination and motivation, effective planning and goal setting are necessary but ultimately insufficient for us to triumphantly complete this mortal journey. Truly, we must come to rely upon "the merits, and mercy, and grace of the Holy Messiah" (2 Nephi 2:8).

GRACE AND THE ENABLING POWER OF THE ATONEMENT OF JESUS CHRIST

In the Bible Dictionary we learn that the word *grace* frequently is used in the scriptures to connote enabling power:

"[*Grace* is] a word that occurs frequently in the New Testament, especially in the writings of Paul. The main idea of the word is *divine means of help or strength,* given through the bounteous mercy and love of Jesus Christ.

"It is through the grace of the Lord Jesus, made possible by his atoning sacrifice, that mankind will be raised in immortality, every person receiving his body from the grave in a condition of everlasting life. *It is likewise through the grace of the Lord that individuals,* through faith in the atonement of Jesus Christ and repentance of their sins, *receive strength and assistance to do good works that they otherwise would not be able to maintain if left to their own means. This grace is an enabling power* that allows men and women to lay hold on eternal life and exaltation after they have expended their own best efforts" (Bible Dictionary, s.v. "Grace"; emphasis added).

Grace is the divine assistance or heavenly help each of us desperately needs to pursue perfection and qualify for the celestial kingdom. Thus, the enabling power of Christ's Atonement strengthens us to do and be good and to serve beyond our own individual desire and natural capacity.

In my personal scripture study, I often insert the term *enabling power* when I encounter the word *grace*. Consider, for example, this verse with which we are all familiar: "We know that it is by grace that we are saved, after all we can do" (2 Nephi 25:23). I believe we can learn much about this vital aspect of the Atonement if we will insert "enabling and strengthening power" each time we find the word *grace* in the scriptures.

Grace and the Enabling Power: Illustrations and Implications

The journey of mortality is to go from bad to good to better and to have our very natures changed. The Book of Mormon is replete with examples of disciples and prophets who knew, understood, and were transformed by the enabling power of the Atonement in making that journey. As we come to better understand this sacred power, our gospel perspective will be greatly enlarged and enriched. Such a perspective will change us in remarkable ways.

Nephi is an example of one who knew, understood, and relied upon the enabling power of the Savior. Recall that the sons of Lehi had returned to Jerusalem to enlist Ishmael and his household in their cause. Laman and others in the party traveling with Nephi from Jerusalem back to the wilderness rebelled, and Nephi exhorted his brethren to have faith in the Lord. It was at this point in their journey that Nephi's brothers bound him with cords and planned his destruction. Please note Nephi's prayer: "O Lord, according to my faith which is in thee, wilt thou deliver me from the hands of my brethren; yea, even *give me strength that I may burst these bands* with which I am bound" (1 Nephi 7:17; emphasis added).

Do you know what I likely would have prayed for if my

NOTES

brothers had tied me up? "Please get me out of this mess NOW!"
It is especially interesting to me that Nephi did not pray to have
his circumstances changed. Rather, he prayed for the strength to
change his circumstances. And I believe he prayed and asked in
faith in this manner precisely because he knew, understood, and
had experienced the enabling power of the Savior made possible
through His Atonement.

I personally do not think the bands with which Nephi was
bound just magically fell from his hands and wrists. Rather, I suspect he was blessed with both persistence and personal strength
beyond his natural capacity, that he then "in the strength of the
Lord" (Mosiah 9:17) worked and twisted and tugged on the cords,
and ultimately and literally was enabled to break the bands.

The implication of this episode for each of us is straightforward. As you and I come to understand and employ the enabling
power of the Atonement in our personal lives, we will pray and
seek for strength to change our circumstances rather than praying
for our circumstances to be changed. We will become agents who
act rather than objects that are acted upon (see 2 Nephi 2:14).

Consider the example recorded in the Book of Mormon of Alma
and his people, who were being persecuted by Amulon. The voice of
the Lord came to these good people in their affliction and indicated:

"I will also ease the burdens which are put upon your shoul-
ders, that even you cannot feel them upon your backs. . . .

"And now it came to pass that the burdens which were laid
upon Alma and his brethren were made light; yea, *the Lord did
strengthen them* that they could bear up their burdens with ease,
and they did submit cheerfully and with patience to all the will of
the Lord" (Mosiah 24:14–15; emphasis added).

What was changed in this episode? The burden was not
changed; the challenges and difficulties of persecution were not

immediately removed from the people. But Alma and his followers were strengthened, and their increased capacity and strength made the burdens they bore lighter. These good people were empowered through the Atonement to *act* as agents and imp*act* their circumstances. And "in the strength of the Lord" Alma and his people were then directed to safety in the land of Zarahemla.

You legitimately may be wondering, "What makes the episode with Alma and his people an example of the enabling power of the Atonement?" The answer is found in a comparison of Mosiah 3:19 and Mosiah 24:15.

"And putteth off the natural man and becometh a saint through the atonement of Christ the Lord, and *becometh as a child, submissive, meek, humble, patient, full of love, willing to submit to all things which the Lord* seeth *fit to inflict upon him,* even as a child doth submit to his father" (Mosiah 3:19; emphasis added).

As we progress in the journey of mortality from bad to good to better, as we put off the natural man or woman in each of us, and as we strive to become saints and have our very natures changed, then the Christlike attributes detailed in this verse increasingly should describe the type of person you and I are becoming. We will become more childlike, more humble, more patient, and more willing to submit.

Now compare these characteristics in Mosiah 3:19 with those used to describe Alma and his people: "And they did *submit* cheerfully and *with patience to all the will of the Lord*" (Mosiah 24:15; emphasis added).

I find the parallels between the attributes described in these verses striking and an indication that Alma's good people were becoming a better people through the enabling power of the Atonement of Christ the Lord.

Recall the story of Alma the Younger and Amulek contained

in Alma 14. In this incident many faithful Saints had been put to death by fire, and these two servants of the Lord had been imprisoned and beaten. Consider this petition offered by Alma as he prayed in prison: "O Lord, *give us strength* according to our faith which is in Christ, even unto deliverance" (Alma 14:26; emphasis added).

Here again we see Alma's understanding of and confidence in the enabling power of the Savior reflected in his request. And note the result of this prayer:

"And they [Alma and Amulek] broke the cords with which they were bound; and when the people saw this, they began to flee, for the fear of destruction had come upon them. . . .

"And Alma and Amulek came forth out of the prison, and they were not hurt; for *the Lord had granted unto them power,* according to their faith which was in Christ" (Alma 14:26, 28; emphasis added).

Once again the enabling power is evident as good people struggle against evil and strive to become even better and serve more effectively "in the strength of the Lord."

Another example from the Book of Mormon is instructive. As recorded in Alma 31, Alma directed a mission to reclaim the apostate Zoramites, who, after building their Rameumptom, offered a prescribed and prideful prayer.

Notice the plea for strength in Alma's personal prayer: "O Lord, wilt thou grant unto me *that I may have strength,* that I may suffer with patience these afflictions which shall come upon me, because of the iniquity of this people" (Alma 31:31; emphasis added).

Alma also prayed that his missionary companions would receive a similar blessing: "Wilt thou grant unto them *that they may have strength,* that they may bear their afflictions which shall come upon them because of the iniquities of this people" (Alma 31:33; emphasis added).

Alma did not pray to have his afflictions removed. He knew he was an agent of the Lord, and he prayed for the power to act and affect his situation.

The key point of this example is contained in the final verse of Alma 31: "[The Lord] gave them strength, that they should suffer no manner of afflictions, *save it were swallowed up in the joy of Christ.* Now this was according to the prayer of Alma; and this because he prayed in faith" (verse 38; emphasis added).

The afflictions were not removed. But Alma and his companions were strengthened and blessed through the enabling power of the Atonement to "suffer no manner of afflictions, save it were swallowed up in the joy of Christ." What a marvelous blessing. And what a lesson each of us should learn.

Examples of the enabling power are not restricted to the scriptures. Daniel W. Jones was born in 1830 in Missouri, and he joined the Church in California in 1851. In 1856 he participated in the rescue of handcart companies that were stranded in Wyoming by severe snowstorms. After the rescue party had found the suffering Saints, provided what immediate comfort they could, and made arrangements for the sick and the feeble to be transported to Salt Lake City, Daniel and several other young men volunteered to remain with and safeguard the company's possessions. The food and supplies left with Daniel and his colleagues were meager and rapidly expended. The following quote from Daniel Jones's personal journal describes the events that followed.

"Game soon became so scarce that we could kill nothing. We ate all the poor meat; one would get hungry eating it. Finally that was all gone, nothing now but hides were left. We made a trial of them. A lot was cooked and eaten without any seasoning and it made the whole company sick. . . .

"Things looked dark, for nothing remained but the poor raw hides taken from starved cattle. We asked the Lord to direct us what to do. The brethren did not murmur, but felt to trust in God. . . . Finally I was impressed how to fix the stuff and gave the company advice, telling them how to cook it; for them to scorch and scrape the hair off; this had a tendency to kill and purify the bad taste that scalding gave it. After scraping, boil one hour in plenty of water, throwing the water away which had extracted all the glue, then wash and scrape the hide thoroughly, washing in cold water, then boil to a jelly and let it get cold, and then eat with a little sugar sprinkled on it. This was considerable trouble, but we had little else to do and it was better than starving.

"We asked the Lord to bless our stomachs and *adapt them to this food.* . . . On eating now all seemed to relish the feast. We were three days without eating before this second attempt was made. We enjoyed this sumptuous fare for about six weeks" (*Forty Years among the Indians,* 57–58; emphasis added).

In those circumstances I probably would have prayed for something else to eat: "Heavenly Father, please send me a quail or a buffalo." It likely would not have occurred to me to pray that my stomach would be strengthened and adapted to the food available to us. What did Daniel W. Jones know? He knew about the enabling power of the Atonement of Jesus Christ. He did not pray that his circumstances would be changed. He prayed that he would be strengthened to deal with his circumstances. Just as Alma and his people, Alma the Younger, Amulek, and Nephi were strengthened, Daniel W. Jones had the spiritual insight to know what to ask for in that prayer.

The enabling power of the Atonement of Christ strengthens us to do things we could never do on our own. Sometimes I wonder, in our latter-day world of ease—with microwave ovens and cell phones and air-conditioned cars and comfortable homes—if we ever learn to acknowledge our daily dependence upon the enabling power of the Atonement.

My wife, Susan, is a remarkably faithful and competent woman, and I have learned important lessons about the strengthening power from her quiet example. I watched her persevere through intense and continuous morning sickness. She was literally sick all day every day for eight months during each of her three pregnancies. Together we prayed that she would be blessed, but that challenge was never removed. Instead, she was enabled and strengthened to do physically what she could not do in her own power. Over the years I have also watched how she has been magnified to handle the mocking and scorn that come from a secular society when a Latter-day Saint woman heeds prophetic counsel and makes the family and the nurturing of children her highest priorities.

Susan's experiences with the strengthening power of the Atonement are particularly powerful precisely because they may seem to be rather common and ordinary. These simple episodes bear eloquent testimony of the truth that the blessings of the Savior's Atonement are available to and efficacious for all of us in our every-day challenges and struggles. "Of a truth . . . God is no respecter of persons" (Acts 10:34; see also Doctrine and Covenants 1:35; 38:16).

I thank and pay tribute to Susan for helping me to learn such vital spiritual truths.

THE SAVIOR KNOWS AND UNDERSTANDS

In Alma chapter 7 we learn why and how the Savior is able to provide the enabling power.

"He shall go forth, suffering *pains* and *afflictions* and *temptations* of every kind; and this that the word might be fulfilled which saith he will take upon him the *pains* and the *sicknesses* of his people.

"And he will take upon him death, that he may loose the bands of death which bind his people; and he will take upon him their *infirmities,* that his bowels may be filled with mercy, according to the flesh, that he may know according to the flesh how to succor his people according to their infirmities" (Alma 7:11–12; emphasis added).

The Savior has suffered not just for our iniquities but also for the inequality, the unfairness, the pain, the anguish, and the emotional distresses that so frequently beset us. There is no physical pain, no anguish of soul, no suffering of spirit, no infirmity or weakness that you or I ever experience during our mortal journey that the Savior did not experience first. You and I in a moment of weakness may cry out, "No one understands. No one knows." No human being, perhaps, knows. But the Son of God perfectly knows and understands, for He felt and bore our burdens before we ever did. And because He paid the ultimate price and bore that burden, He has perfect empathy and can extend to us His arm of mercy in so many phases of our lives. He can reach out, touch, succor—literally run to us—and strengthen us to be more than we could ever be and help us to do that which we could never do relying only upon our individual ability.

"Come unto me, all ye that labour and are heavy laden, and I will give you rest.

"Take my yoke upon you, and learn of me; for I am meek and lowly in heart: and ye shall find rest unto your souls.

"For my yoke is easy, and my burden is light" (Matthew 11:28–30).

A yoke is a wooden beam, normally used between a pair of oxen or other animals, that enables them to pull together on a load when working in pairs. A yoke places animals side by side so they can move together in order to accomplish a task.

Consider the uniquely individual invitation to "take my yoke upon you." Making and keeping sacred covenants yokes us to and with the Lord Jesus Christ. In essence, the Savior is beckoning us to rely upon and pull together with Him, even though our best efforts are not equal to and cannot be compared with His. Christ took upon Himself pains and sicknesses; He took upon Himself death; He took upon Himself infirmities—that "he may know according to the flesh how to succor his people" (Alma 7:12). As we come unto the Savior, trust in and rely upon Him, and pull with Him during the journey of mortality, truly His yoke is easy, and His burden is light (see Matthew 11:30).

We are not and never need be alone. We do not press forward on the pathway to perfection without heavenly help. "Therefore, continue your journey and let your hearts rejoice; for behold, and lo, I am with you even unto the end" (Doctrine and Covenants 100:12).

Through the Savior's Atonement we can receive capacity and find strength beyond our own (see "Lord, I Would Follow Thee," *Hymns,* no. 220). A loving Savior indeed will "lead me, guide me, walk beside me, help me find the way" ("I Am a Child of God," *Hymns,* no. 301).

SUMMARY

As we increase in learning about the attributes and character of the Savior and act in His doctrine, we are blessed with power to become more like Him. We receive grace for grace and are strengthened to do good and to become better through His infinite and eternal Atonement. Our direction on the pathway of perfection becomes increasingly clear and our pace ever more steady. We are blessed to "press forward with a steadfastness in Christ, having a perfect brightness of hope, and a love of God and of all men. Wherefore, if ye shall press forward, feasting upon the word of Christ, and endure to the end, behold, thus saith the Father: Ye shall have eternal life.

"And now, behold, my beloved brethren, this is the way; and there is none other way nor name given under heaven whereby man can be saved in the kingdom of God. And now, behold, this is the doctrine of Christ, and the only and true doctrine of the Father, and of the Son, and of the Holy Ghost, which is one God, without end. Amen" (2 Nephi 31:20–21).

Because the Savior's way "is the way," and because there is "none other way," then we can in mortality obtain an actual knowledge that the course of life we are pursuing is in accordance with God's will (see *Lectures on Faith,* 67).

> *Why should we mourn or think our lot is hard?*
> *'Tis not so; all is right.*
> *Why should we think to earn a great reward*
> *If we now shun the fight?*
> *Gird up your loins; fresh courage take.*
> *Our God will never us forsake;*
> *And soon we'll have this tale to tell—*
> *All is well! All is well!*
> *("Come, Come, Ye Saints," Hymns, no. 30)*

"O then, my beloved brethren, come unto the Lord, the Holy One. Remember that his paths are righteous. Behold, the way for man is narrow, but it lieth in a straight course before him, and the keeper of the gate is the Holy One of Israel; and he employeth no servant there; and there is none other way save it be by the gate" (2 Nephi 9:41).

Related Readings

1. Thomas S. Monson, "He Is Risen!" *Ensign,* May 2010, 87–90.

2. James E. Faust, "The Atonement: Our Greatest Hope," *Ensign,* November 2001, 18–20.

3. Gordon B. Hinckley, "To All the World in Testimony," *Ensign,* May 2000, 4–6.

4. Bruce R. McConkie, "The Purifying Power of Gethsemane," *Ensign,* May 1985, 9–11.

5. Dallin H. Oaks, "Revelation," BYU Devotional, September 29, 1981. Available online at speeches.byu.edu.

6. Spencer W. Kimball, "Absolute Truth," BYU Devotional, September 6, 1977. Available online at speeches.byu.edu.

7. John A. Widtsoe, "The Transforming Power of the Gospel," in Conference Report, April 1952, 32–35.

Explore these concepts further with a group discussion.

Scan this code or visit seek.deseretbook.com/powertobecome

CONSIDER

What can and should I do to invite into my life the strengthening and enabling power of the Atonement of Jesus Christ?

CONSIDER

How does increasing my understanding of the "power to become" affect my heart, my motives, and my behavior?

CONSIDER

What can and should I do in my life to continue pressing forward with steadfastness on the pathway to perfection?

MY OWN QUESTIONS TO CONSIDER

Scriptures Related to What I Am Learning

AN INVITATION TO LEARN, TO ACT, AND TO BECOME		
What additional doctrines and principles, if understood, would help me appropriately invite into my life the power to become?	What can and should I do to act in those doctrines and principles?	How will I know if I am making progress in striving to become more like the Savior?

AN INVITATION TO LEARN, TO ACT, AND TO BECOME		
What additional doctrines and principles, if understood, would help me appropriately invite into my life the power to become?	What can and should I do to act in those doctrines and principles?	How will I know if I am making progress in striving to become more like the Savior?

AN INVITATION TO LEARN, TO ACT, AND TO BECOME		
What additional doctrines and principles, if understood, would help me appropriately invite into my life the power to become?	What can and should I do to act in those doctrines and principles?	How will I know if I am making progress in striving to become more like the Savior?

CHAPTER 2

POWER TO BECOME AND THE
SPIRITUAL GIFT OF PERSONAL PEACE

As we endeavor to live righteously and to appropriately pursue perfection in Christ, we can receive from the Savior, through His Atonement, enlarged capacity, spiritual gifts, and supernal blessings. One of the greatest spiritual gifts we can be given as we press forward along the strait and narrow path is personal peace.

We often encounter obstacles of various kinds and unanticipated delays as we progress along the pathway to perfection in the journey of mortality. However, personal peace provides a perspective, a settledness, and a tranquillity that help us to keep our focus fixed on our eternal destination—in spite of life's challenges and disappointments.

As the Prophet Joseph Smith languished in Liberty Jail from December 1838 to April 1839 along with several other Church leaders, he suffered knowing that the Latter-day Saints were being driven from Missouri under an "extermination order" from the governor. The Prophet cried unto the Lord for understanding and strength.

"O God, where art thou? And where is the pavilion that covereth thy hiding place?

"How long shall thy hand be stayed, and thine eye, yea thy pure eye, behold from the eternal heavens the wrongs of thy people and of thy servants, and thine ear be penetrated with their cries?

"Yea, O Lord, how long shall they suffer these wrongs and unlawful oppressions, before thine heart shall be softened toward them, and thy bowels be moved with compassion toward them?

"O Lord God Almighty, maker of heaven, earth, and seas, and of all things that in them are, and who controllest and subjectest the devil, and the dark and benighted dominion of Sheol—stretch forth thy hand; let thine eye pierce; let thy pavilion be taken up; let thy hiding place no longer be covered; let thine ear be inclined; let thine heart be softened, and thy bowels moved with compassion toward us.

"Let thine anger be kindled against our enemies; and, in the fury of thine heart, with thy sword avenge us of our wrongs.

"Remember thy suffering saints, O our God; and thy servants will rejoice in thy name forever.

"My son, *peace be unto thy soul;* thine adversity and thine afflictions shall be but a small moment;

"And then, if thou endure it well, God shall exalt thee on high; thou shalt triumph over all thy foes" (Doctrine and Covenants 121:1–8; emphasis added).

In the midst of the adversity he and the Saints experienced because of his unjust imprisonment, Joseph Smith learned once again what each of us must learn—that the Lord Jesus Christ is the only source of enduring, personal peace.

"Learn of me, and listen to my words; walk in the meekness of my Spirit, and you shall have peace in me.

"I am Jesus Christ; I came by the will of the Father, and I do his will" (Doctrine and Covenants 19:23–24).

"But learn that he who doeth the works of righteousness shall receive his reward, even peace in this world, and eternal life in the world to come.

"I, the Lord, have spoken it, and the Spirit beareth record. Amen" (Doctrine and Covenants 59:23–24).

"And the peace of God, which passeth all understanding, shall keep your hearts and minds through Christ Jesus" (Philippians 4:7).

The Savior promised His Apostles they would be blessed with the "Comforter, which is the Holy Ghost," and then made this important declaration: "Peace I leave with you, my peace I give unto you: not as the world giveth, give I unto you" (John 14:26–27). Then just before His Intercessory Prayer: "These things I have spoken unto you, that in me ye might have peace. In the world ye shall have tribulation: but be of good cheer; I have overcome the world" (John 16:33).

The peace the Savior bestows upon us as His disciples is a vital component of the power to become ever more like Him, and each of us appropriately must ask and seek for this important blessing. His peace enables us to submit with meekness and as a child—as He did; to endure with perspective and patience—as He did; to bear burdens with humility and dignity—as He did; and to "shrink not" from the bitter cup—as He did. Thus, the spiritual gift of personal peace is the foundation upon which the power to become is established.

The role and importance of personal peace in the journey of mortality are emphasized repeatedly in the teachings of latter-day prophets and apostles.

President Heber J. Grant declared, "His peace will ease our suffering, bind up our broken hearts, blot out our hates, engender in our breasts a love of fellow men that will suffuse our souls with calm and happiness" (*Teachings of Presidents of the Church: Heber J. Grant,* 226).

President George Albert Smith testified, "Though the world may be filled with distress, and the heavens gather blackness, and the vivid lightnings flash, and the earth quake from center to circumference, if we know that God lives, and our lives are righteous, we will be happy, there will be peace unspeakable because we know our Father approves [of] our lives" (*Teachings of Presidents of the Church: George Albert Smith,* 260).

Elder Jeffrey R. Holland testified: "We declare to all the world that for real and abiding peace to come, we must strive to be more like that exemplary Son of God. Many among us are trying to do that. I salute you for your obedience, your forbearance, your waiting faithfully upon the Lord for the strength you seek which will surely come. Some of us, on the other hand, need to make some changes, need to make greater effort in gospel living. And change we can. The very beauty of the word *repentance* is the promise of escaping old problems and old habits and old sorrows and old sins. It is among the most hopeful and encouraging—and yes, most peaceful—words in the gospel vocabulary. In seeking true peace some of us need to improve what has to be improved, confess what needs to be confessed, forgive what has to be forgiven, and forget what should be forgotten in order that serenity can come to us. If there is a commandment we are breaking, and as a result it is breaking us and hurting those who love us, let us call down the power of the Lord Jesus Christ to help us, to free us, to lead us through repentance to that peace 'which passeth all understanding' (Philippians 4:7)" ("'The Peaceable Things of the Kingdom,'" 83).

Truly, as we choose the right there is peace in righteous doing; there is safety for the soul. Choosing the right in all labors we are pursuing will let God and heaven be our goal (see "Choose the Right," *Hymns,* no. 239).

Principles Related to Personal Peace

I am acquainted with a woman whose elderly mother was involved in a serious automobile accident. This loving mother suffered head injuries and severe trauma. Over the course of several days in the hospital, pneumonia set in and this noble matriarch slipped into a semicomatose state. And at one point, the doctors advised the family that she would probably not live through the night.

The daughter stayed at the hospital with her mother that dark and fateful night—joined by an older brother who was less active in the Church. This sister and brother had an opportunity during those sleepless hours to visit about and discuss many things. At one point, the brother said to his sister: "I hope there is a God, and I hope all that Mom believes about Him is true. She has lived her entire life to that end." The daughter recalls standing in that hospital room and having a calm, peaceful reassurance encircle her—a witness that, indeed, all that her mother believed about her God was true: that life goes on beyond mortality; that families can be together forever; that her mother's God knew of her situation and would not forsake her.

How grateful the daughter was for what she felt and experienced in the hospital! Her mother did not pass away that night. Rather, she was permitted to live and bless that family with her association for another eight months. However, those were not easy months for this caring daughter and her devoted siblings. The mother they had known before the accident never really came back to them, and the family was presented with difficult challenges and decisions. Repeatedly, the faithful daughter found herself drawing upon the experience in the hospital as a source of strength and comfort. Truly, this good woman came to understand what the Savior meant when He said, "Peace I leave with you, my peace I give unto you. . . . Let not your heart be troubled, neither let it be afraid" (John 14:27).

I have a friend who recalls a fateful day in early June when she was twelve years old. Her father had passed away earlier that morning after having suffered with cancer for a relatively short period of time. The mortician had taken away his body, and friends and family were beginning to call and stop by the house. She remembers thinking there was too much commotion and feeling confused and very much afraid.

At some point, probably about midday, this little girl found herself sitting in the room where her father had died, his hospital bed now empty. She was sitting on the edge of the other bed in the room looking out the window across the front yard. The day was dreary. It had been raining for days—or so it seemed. Suddenly a ray of sunlight managed to cut through the clouds and glistened on the wet grass. At the same time, a ray of hope managed to find its way into the heart of a young girl. She was filled with an assurance that all was well with her father. She knew he was alive! And she knew that all would be well with her and with her mother and with her brothers and sisters. This young woman felt the peace offered by the Savior when He said, "Peace I leave with you, my peace I give unto you: not as the world giveth, give I unto you. Let not your heart be troubled, neither let it be afraid." The heart of this child was no longer troubled; she was no longer confused or afraid.

The Savior's peace is potent, and it is available in a wide variety of situations and circumstances. For example, one of the greatest war stories in the Book of Mormon is contained in chapters 56 through 58 in the book of Alma. Helaman had taken the command over 2,000 young Lamanites whose parents had sworn never to take up arms against their enemies. But their sons, who had not taken the oath, placed themselves under Helaman's direction and helped the Nephites in their critical battles against the Lamanites. Because of their remarkable faith and ability, these young men were instrumental in helping to defend the rights of the Nephite people.

Verses 10 through 13 in chapter 58 are especially instructive about the role of prayer in the preparations of these young men for war—and about the specific type of spiritual help they received.

"Therefore we did pour out our souls in prayer to God, that he would strengthen us and deliver us out of the hands of our enemies, yea, and also give us strength that we might retain our cities, and our lands, and our possessions, for the support of our people."

Note the blessings the young warriors received in response to their prayers, as described in verses 11 and 12 and the beginning of verse 13.

"Yea, and it came to pass that the Lord our God did visit us with *assurances* that he would deliver us; yea, insomuch that he did speak *peace to our souls,* and did grant unto us *great faith,* and did cause us that we should *hope* for our deliverance in him.

"And we did take *courage* with our small force which we had received, and were fixed with a *determination* to conquer our enemies, and to maintain our lands, and our possessions, and our wives, and our children, and the cause of our liberty.

"And thus *we did go forth with all our might* against the Lamanites" (emphasis added).

Interestingly, the answers to these prayers did not produce additional weapons or an increased number of troops. Instead, God granted these faithful warriors assurance He would deliver them, peace to their souls, and great faith and hope. Thus, the sons of Helaman did take courage, were fixed with a determination to conquer, and did go forth with all of their might against the Lamanites. Assurance, personal peace, faith, and hope initially might not seem like the blessings warriors in battle might want, but they were precisely the blessings these valiant young men needed to press forward and prevail physically and spiritually. These faithful and stalwart young men undoubtedly were learning what the Savior meant when He said, "Peace I leave with you, my peace I give unto you. . . . Let not your heart be troubled, neither let it be afraid" (John 14:27).

A small six-year-old boy was participating in a ward activity, a water party. At one point during the afternoon, the little boy decided to lie down on the blacktop of the parking lot to dry off. A neighbor and fellow ward member accidentally ran over the boy, killing him almost instantly.

As the little boy's mother knelt over his lifeless body, she found the following questions racing through her mind: "Oh, son, why would you lie down on the blacktop? Why did you not move when you heard the car start?" A thought then came into the mind of that sorrowing mother almost as quickly as the questions had come: "If he could answer me, he would say: 'Mom, it does not even matter. It just does not matter.'"

In those initial moments after losing her son, this woman was blessed with the peace promised by the Savior—the assurance that, in the eternal scheme of things, the questions she had asked simply did not matter. Her son had been transferred into another phase of his eternal existence, and the specific process by which that transfer came to pass simply did not matter. This young mother was experiencing what the Savior meant when He said, "Peace I leave with you, my peace I give unto you. . . . Let not your heart be troubled, neither let it be afraid."

As I have reflected upon these stories and many similar ones, I have been impressed by three recurring principles related to peace: (1) peace is centered in Christ, (2) faith and hope in the Savior invite the spiritual gift of peace into our lives—the peace that only the Prince of Peace can offer, and (3) the peace Christ gives to us passeth all understanding.

Principle 1: Peace is centered in Christ.

The world searches to and fro for peace and often believes personal fulfillment is to be found in material possessions, in prestige and prominence, or in the interpersonal advice so readily dispensed in the self-help section of a local bookstore. Such approaches to finding peace wholly and totally miss the mark—which is the Lord Jesus Christ.

The Book of Mormon teaches about two basic kinds of peace: civil and spiritual. Civil peace, which is the absence of physical and social conflict, was much desired and sought after by the righteous peoples described in the Book of Mormon. Of even greater value, however, is the spiritual peace or "peace of conscience" that is granted to faithful individuals by the Holy Ghost through application of the Atonement of the Lord Jesus Christ. Peace originates in Christ and comes from and because of Christ. And it is imperative that we remember this: it is His peace that He gives to us.

In Mosiah, chapter 4, we learn about the reaction of King

Benjamin's people to his sermon about the Savior and His Atonement. We also learn that true peace of conscience is centered in the Redeemer and flows from His infinite Atonement.

"And now, it came to pass that when king Benjamin had made an end of speaking the words which had been delivered unto him by the angel of the Lord, that he cast his eyes round about on the multitude, and behold they had fallen to the earth, for the fear of the Lord had come upon them.

"And they had viewed themselves in their own carnal state, even less than the dust of the earth. And they all cried aloud with one voice, saying: O have mercy, and apply the atoning blood of Christ that we may receive *forgiveness of our sins,* and *our hearts may be purified;* for we believe in Jesus Christ, the Son of God, who created heaven and earth, and all things; who shall come down among the children of men.

"And it came to pass that after they had spoken these words the Spirit of the Lord came upon them, and they were *filled with joy,* having received a remission of their sins, and *having peace of conscience,* because of the exceeding faith which they had in Jesus Christ who should come, according to the words which King Benjamin had spoken unto them" (Mosiah 4:1–3; emphasis added).

Please note the relationship between obtaining a remission of sins and experiencing joy, and between having our hearts purified and receiving peace of conscience. Only the atoning blood of Christ makes both of these sweet spiritual outcomes possible.

As we learn of Christ and listen to His words and walk in the meekness of His spirit, we can indeed receive the peace that only the Prince of Peace can give (see Doctrine and Covenants 19:23).

Principle 2: Faith and hope in the Savior invite
the spiritual gift of peace into our lives.

How can a woman watching her mother struggle through serious injuries and an extensive period of rehabilitation receive ongoing strength and spiritual reassurance? How does a twelve-year-old girl who is struggling to understand the death of her father come to know that all is well—with her father and with her mother and siblings? How could the stripling warriors march forward with a determination to conquer—even when tremendously outnumbered and facing a ferocious enemy? How can a young mother feel a sense of reassurance even in the first moments following the death of her young son? And how can each of us receive the gift of personal peace in the rather routine but nonetheless persistent pressures of our daily lives?

I believe the answers to these penetrating questions are found in Moroni 7:40–42. Please notice in these verses the interrelationship between the principles of faith and hope.

"And again, my beloved brethren, I would speak unto you concerning hope. How is it that ye can attain unto faith, save ye shall have hope?

"And what is it that ye shall hope for? Behold I say unto you that ye shall have hope through the atonement of Christ and the power of his resurrection, to be raised unto life eternal, and this because of your faith in him according to the promise.

"Wherefore, if a man have faith he must needs have hope; for without faith there cannot be any hope."

These verses outline a pattern that invites the gift of peace into our lives. Faith in the Lord Jesus Christ—that is, total trust in Him, complete confidence in Him, and a ready reliance on His merits, mercy, and grace—leads to hope. Because of the Savior's

Atonement, that hope in the power of the Resurrection and in eternal life invites the sweet peace of conscience for which men and women have always yearned. The redeeming and cleansing power of the Savior's Atonement helps us to dispel the despair caused by transgression and sin. And the enabling and strengthening aspect of the Atonement helps us to see and to do and to become good in ways that we could never recognize or accomplish with our limited mortal capacity. As we work and learn and progress and struggle, we are blessed to learn that "he who doeth the works of righteousness shall receive his reward, even peace in this world, and eternal life in the world to come" (Doctrine and Covenants 59:23).

Principle 3: The peace Christ gives to us passeth all understanding.

As I was discussing the topic of peace with family and friends, I was struck by how many times important and even dramatic life events were mentioned—events such as the death of a loved one, the birth of a child, the struggle with physical pain and limitation, or the pivotal nature of a family or career decision. It was particularly interesting that the experience of losing a loved one to death was mentioned most frequently. Now, we recognize and know that receiving the spiritual gift of peace is not solely associated with life-changing and emotional events; we frequently are blessed with peace of conscience in small and simple and seemingly insignificant ways. Nevertheless, I wondered why my questions about peace elicited such consistent responses related to the most difficult and demanding episodes of life.

But the reasons are quite straightforward. Peace is centered in the Lord Jesus Christ. Faith and hope in the Savior invite the spiritual gift of peace into our lives. Our understanding of the plan of happiness and of the role of the infinite and eternal Atonement allows us to see somewhat beyond the boundaries and limitations of mortality. And when we are then confronted with the greatest challenges of our mortal existence, a loving Savior grants unto us a peace that extends beyond mortality and into eternity. It is a peace of conscience that cannot be comprehended in earthly or rational terms. As Paul explained to the Philippians:

"Be careful for nothing; but in every thing by prayer and supplication with thanksgiving let your requests be made known unto God.

"And the peace of God, which passeth all understanding, shall keep your hearts and minds through Christ Jesus" (Philippians 4:6–7).

The daughter who cared for her ailing mother was strengthened by the knowledge that her mother would be resurrected and have a perfected and glorified body and live eternally. The twelve-year-old girl who lost her father received help from heaven to know that, truly, families can and will be together forever as they are true and faithful to their ordinances and covenants. The sons of Helaman were strengthened to fight with firmness and a conviction born of faith in Christ and in the eternal correctness of their cause. And the mother who lost her six-year-old son knew in her heart—in a way that could not necessarily be fully understood in her mind—that "those that die in me shall not taste of death, for it shall be sweet unto them" (Doctrine and Covenants 42:46).

When words cannot provide the solace we need or seek, when it is simply futile to attempt to explain that which is unexplainable, when logic and reason cannot yield adequate understanding of the injustices and inequities of life, when mortal experience and analysis are insufficient, and when it seems that perhaps we are so

NOTES

totally alone, then comes the peace that only the Prince of Peace can give—truly, a peace that passeth all understanding.

Joshua Loth Liebman, in his book *Peace of Mind,* made an inventory as a young man of the things he thought would be most desirable in life—things like health and love, beauty and talent, riches and fame. He showed his list to an older man whom he respected with the assessment that a person who possessed all of these things "would be as a god."

He writes: "At the corners of my friend's old eyes, I saw wrinkles of amusement gathering in a patient net. 'An excellent list,' he said, pondering it thoughtfully. 'Well digested in content and set down in not-unreasonable order. But it appears, my young friend, that you have omitted the most important element of all. You have forgotten the one ingredient lacking which each possession becomes a hideous torment, and your list as a whole an intolerable burden.'

"'And what,' I asked, peppering my voice with truculence, 'is that missing ingredient?'

"With a pencil stub he crossed out my entire schedule. Then, having demolished my adolescent dream structure at a single stroke, he wrote down three syllables: *peace of mind.*"

The wise older friend went on to point out that all the other items on the list were available to many, but that peace of mind was rare indeed, a gift that most people would seek for in vain all their lives.

"At that time I found it difficult wholly to believe the wisdom of my rabbinic friend. But a quarter of a century of personal experience and professional observation has served only to confirm his almost oracular utterance. I have come to understand that peace of mind is the characteristic mark of God Himself. . . . I know now that the sum of all other possessions does not necessarily add up to

peace of mind: yet, on the other hand, I have seen this inner tran-
quility flourish without the material supports of property or even
the buttress of physical health. Slowly, painfully, I have learned
that peace of mind may transform a cottage into a spacious manor
hall; the want of it can make a regal park an imprisoning nutshell"
(*Peace of Mind*, 3–5).

"Peace I leave with you, my peace I give unto you: not as the
world giveth, give I unto you. Let not your heart be troubled, neither let it be afraid" (John 14:27).

Personal peace is centered in Christ. In a world that grows ever
more tumultuous and troubled and unsettled, we can be blessed
with peace of conscience and a clear sense of purpose and direction. The spiritual gifts of faith and hope in the Savior invite the
companion gift of peace into our lives. The peace Christ gives to us
is sweet and reassuring and passeth all understanding.

Peace and Adversity

The personal peace that comes into our lives through faith in
the Lord Jesus Christ can strengthen us to face, overcome, and
learn from adversity. "These things I have spoken unto you, that in
me ye might have peace. In the world ye shall have tribulation: but
be of good cheer; I have overcome the world" (John 16:33).

The following examples demonstrate powerfully the truth that
"to be spiritually minded is life and peace" (Romans 8:6)—and
how the spiritual gift of personal peace is essential for us to become
what God intends for us to become.

A Devoted Disciple and "Not Shrinking"

Elder Neal A. Maxwell was a beloved disciple of the Lord
Jesus Christ. He served as a member of the Quorum of the Twelve

Apostles for twenty-three years, from 1981 to 2004. The spiritual power of his teachings and his example of faithful discipleship blessed and continue to bless in marvelous ways the members of the Savior's restored Church and the people of the world.

In October 1997, Susan and I hosted Elder and Sister Maxwell at Brigham Young University–Idaho. Elder Maxwell was to speak to the students, staff, and faculty in a devotional assembly. Everyone on the campus eagerly anticipated his visit to the university and earnestly prepared to receive his message.

Earlier in that same year, Elder Maxwell had undergone forty-six days and nights of debilitating chemotherapy for leukemia. Shortly after completing his treatments and being released from the hospital, he spoke briefly in the April general conference of the Church. His rehabilitation and continued therapy progressed positively through the spring and summer months, but Elder Maxwell's physical strength and stamina were nonetheless limited when he traveled to Rexburg. After greeting Elder and Sister Maxwell at the airport, Susan and I drove them to our home for rest and a light lunch before the devotional.

During the course of our conversations that day, I asked Elder Maxwell what lessons he had learned through his illness. I will remember always the precise and penetrating answer he gave. "Dave," he said, "I have learned that not shrinking is more important than surviving."

His response to my inquiry was a principle with which he had gained extensive personal experience during his chemotherapy. As Elder Maxwell and his wife were driving to the hospital in January 1997, on the day he was scheduled to begin his first round of treatment, they pulled into the parking lot and paused for a private moment together. Elder Maxwell "breathed a deep sigh and looked at [his wife]. He reached for her hand and said, 'I just don't

NOTES

want to *shrink*'" (Bruce C. Hafen, *A Disciple's Life,* 16; emphasis in original).

In his October 1997 general conference message, Elder Maxwell taught with great authenticity: "As we confront our own . . . trials and tribulations, we too can plead with the Father, just as Jesus did, that we 'might not . . . shrink'—meaning to retreat or to recoil (D&C 19:18). Not shrinking is much more important than surviving! Moreover, partaking of a bitter cup without becoming bitter is likewise part of the emulation of Jesus" ("'Apply the Atoning Blood of Christ,'" 22).

Elder Maxwell's answer to my question caused me to reflect on the teachings of Elder Orson F. Whitney, who also served as a member of the Quorum of the Twelve Apostles: "No pain that we suffer, no trial that we experience is wasted. It ministers to our education, to the development of such qualities as patience, faith, fortitude and humility. All that we suffer and all that we endure, especially when we endure it patiently, builds up our characters, purifies our hearts, expands our souls, and makes us more tender and charitable, more worthy to be called the children of God . . . and it is through sorrow and suffering, toil and tribulation, that we gain the education that we come here to acquire" (quoted in Spencer W. Kimball, *Faith Precedes the Miracle,* 98).

And these scriptures concerning the Savior's suffering as He offered the infinite and eternal atoning sacrifice became even more poignant and meaningful to me.

"Therefore I command you to repent—repent, lest I smite you by the rod of my mouth, and by my wrath, and by my anger, and your sufferings be sore—how sore you know not, how exquisite you know not, yea, how hard to bear you know not.

"For behold, I, God, have suffered these things for all, that they might not suffer if they would repent;

"But if they would not repent they must suffer even as I;

"Which suffering caused myself, even God, the greatest of all, to tremble because of pain, and to bleed at every pore, and to suffer both body and spirit—and would that I might not drink the bitter cup, and shrink—

"Nevertheless, glory be to the Father, and I partook and finished my preparations unto the children of men" (Doctrine and Covenants 19:15–19).

The Savior did not shrink in Gethsemane or on Golgotha.

Elder Maxwell also did not shrink. This mighty Apostle pressed forward steadfastly and was blessed with additional time in mortality to love, to serve, to teach, and to testify. Those concluding years of his life were an emphatic exclamation point to his example of devoted discipleship—through both his words and his deeds.

I believe most of us likely would expect a man with the spiritual capacity, experience, and stature of Elder Maxwell to face serious illness and death with an understanding of God's plan of happiness, with assurance and grace, and with personal peace of conscience. And he surely did. But I bear witness that such blessings are not reserved exclusively for General Authorities or for a select few members of the Church.

Since my call to fill the vacancy in the Quorum of the Twelve created by the death of Elder Maxwell, my assignments and travels have enabled me to become acquainted with faithful, courageous, and valiant Latter-day Saints all over the world. One young man and one young woman have been a particular blessing in my life, and together we have learned spiritually vital lessons about not shrinking and about allowing our individual wills to be "swallowed up in the will of the Father" (Mosiah 15:7).

The account that follows is true, and the characters are real. I will not, however, use the actual names of the individuals who are involved. I refer to the young man as John and the young woman as Heather. I also use with permission selected statements from their personal journals.

The Faith Not to Be Healed

John is a worthy priesthood holder and served faithfully as a full-time missionary. After returning home from his mission, he dated and married a righteous and wonderful young woman, Heather. John was twenty-three and Heather was twenty on the day they were sealed together for time and for all eternity in the house of the Lord. Please keep in mind the respective ages of John and Heather as this story unfolds.

Approximately three weeks after their temple marriage, John was diagnosed with bone cancer. As cancer nodules also were discovered in his lungs, the prognosis was not good.

John recorded in his journal: "This was the scariest day of my life. Not only because I was told I had cancer, but also because I was newly married and somehow felt that I had failed as a husband. I was the provider and protector of our new family, and now—three weeks into that role—I felt like I had failed. I know that thought is absurd, but it is one of the crazy things I told myself in a moment of crisis."

Heather noted: "This was devastating news, and I remember how greatly it changed our perspectives. I was in a hospital waiting room writing wedding thank you notes as we anticipated the results of [John's] tests. But after learning about [John's] cancer, crock-pots and cookware did not seem so important anymore. This was the worst day of my life, but I remember going to bed that night with gratitude for our temple sealing. Though the doctors had given [John] only a 30 percent chance of survival, I knew that if we remained faithful I had a 100 percent chance to be with him forever."

Approximately one month later, John began chemotherapy. He described his experience: "The treatments caused me to be sicker than I had ever been in my life. I lost my hair, dropped 41 pounds, and my body felt like it was falling apart. The chemotherapy also affected me emotionally, mentally, and spiritually. Life was a roller coaster during the months of chemo with highs, lows, and everything in between. But through it all, [Heather] and I maintained the faith that God would heal me. We just knew it."

Heather chronicled her thoughts and feelings: "I could not stand to let [John] spend the night alone in the hospital, so I would sleep every night on the small couch in his room. We had lots of friends and family visit during the day, but the nights were the hardest. I would stare at the ceiling and wonder what Heavenly Father had planned for us. Sometimes my mind would wander into dark places, and my fear of losing [John] would almost overtake me. But I knew these thoughts were not from Heavenly Father. My prayers for comfort became more frequent, and the Lord gave me the strength to keep going."

Three months later, John underwent a surgical procedure to remove a large tumor in his leg. John stated: "The surgery was a huge deal for us because pathology tests were to be run on the tumor to see how much of it was viable and how much of the cancer was dead. This analysis would give us the first indication of the effectiveness of the chemotherapy and of how aggressive we would need to be with future treatments."

Two days following the operation, I visited John and Heather in the hospital. We talked about the first time I had met John in the mission field, about their marriage, about the cancer, and about the eternally important lessons we learn through the trials of mortality.

As we concluded our time together, John asked if I would give him a priesthood blessing. I responded that I gladly would give such a blessing, but I first needed to ask some questions.

I then posed questions I had not planned to ask and had never previously considered: "John, do you have the faith not to be healed? If it is the will of our Heavenly Father that you are transferred by death in your youth to the spirit world to continue your ministry, do you have the faith to submit to His will and not be healed?"

I frankly was surprised by the questions I felt prompted to ask this particular couple. Frequently, as recorded in the scriptures, the Savior or His servants exercised the spiritual gift of healing (see 1 Corinthians 12:9; Doctrine and Covenants 35:9; 46:20) and perceived that an individual had the faith to be healed (see Acts 14:9; 3 Nephi 17:8; Doctrine and Covenants 46:19). But as John and Heather and I counseled together and wrestled with these questions, we increasingly understood that if God's will were for this good young man to be healed, then that blessing could be received only if this valiant couple first had the faith not to be healed. In other words, John and Heather needed to overcome, through the Atonement of the Lord Jesus Christ, the "natural man" (Mosiah 3:19) tendency in all of us to demand impatiently and insist incessantly on the blessings we want and believe we deserve.

We recognized a principle that applies to every devoted disciple: strong faith in the Savior includes submissively accepting His will and timing in our lives—even if the outcome is not what we hoped for or wanted. Certainly, John and Heather would desire, yearn, and plead for healing with all of their might, mind, and strength. But more important, they would be "willing to submit to all things which the Lord seeth fit to inflict upon [them], even as a child doth submit to his father" (Mosiah 3:19). Indeed, they would be willing to "offer [their] whole souls as an offering unto him" (Omni 1:26) and humbly pray, "Father, if thou be willing, remove this cup from me: nevertheless not my will, but thine, be done" (Luke 22:42).

What initially seemed to John, Heather, and me to be perplexing questions became part of a pervasive pattern of gospel paradoxes. Consider the admonition of the Savior: "He that findeth his life shall lose it: and he that loseth his life for my sake shall find it" (Matthew 10:39). He also declared, "But many that are first shall be last; and the last shall be first" (Matthew 19:30). The Lord counseled His latter-day disciples, "By thy word many high ones shall be brought low, and by thy word many low ones shall be exalted" (Doctrine and Covenants 112:8). And He instructed His ancient disciples that they could have personal peace in the midst of tribulation (see John 16:33). Thus, having the faith to not be healed seemed to fit appropriately into a powerful pattern of penetrating paradoxes that require us to ask, to seek, and to knock that we might receive knowledge and understanding (see 3 Nephi 14:7).

After taking the necessary time to ponder my inquiries and to talk with his wife, John said to me: "Elder Bednar, I do not want to die. I do not want to leave Heather. But if the will of the Lord is to transfer me to the spirit world, then I guess I am good with that." My heart swelled with appreciation and admiration as I witnessed this young couple confronting the most demanding of all spiritual struggles—the submissive surrender of their wills to God's will. My faith was strengthened as I witnessed them allowing their strong and understandable desires for healing to be "swallowed up in the will of the Father" (Mosiah 15:7).

John described his reaction to our conversation and the blessing he received: "Elder Bednar shared with us the thought from

Elder Maxwell that it is better to not shrink than to survive. Elder Bednar then asked us, 'I know you have the faith to be healed, but do you have the faith not to be healed?' This was a foreign concept to me. Essentially he was asking if I had the faith to accept God's will if His will were that I not be healed? If the time were approaching for me to enter the spirit world through death, was I prepared to submit and accept?"

John continued: "Having the faith not to be healed seemed counterintuitive; but that perspective changed the way my wife and I thought and allowed us to put our trust fully in the Father's plan for us. We learned we needed to gain the faith that the Lord is in charge whatever the outcome may be, and He will guide us from where we are to where we need to be. As we prayed, our petitions changed from 'Please make me whole' to 'Please give me the faith to accept whatever outcome Thou hast planned for me.'

"I was sure that since Elder Bednar was an Apostle, he would bless the elements of my body to realign, and I would jump out of the bed and start to dance or do something dramatic like that! But as he blessed me that day, I was amazed that the words he spoke were almost identical to those of my father, my father-in-law, and my mission president. I realized that ultimately it does not matter whose hands are on my head. God's power does not change, and His will is made known to us individually and through His authorized servants."

Heather wrote: "This day was filled with mixed emotions for me. I was convinced that Elder Bednar would place his hands on [John's] head and completely heal him of the cancer. I knew that through the power of the priesthood he could be healed, and I wanted so bad for that to happen. After he taught us about the faith to not be healed, I was terrified. Up to that point, I had never had to come to grips with the fact that the Lord's plan might include losing my new husband. My faith was dependent upon the out-comes I wanted. In a manner of speaking, it was one-dimensional. Though terrifying at first, the thought of having the faith not to be healed ultimately freed me from worry. It allowed me to have complete trust that my Heavenly Father knew me better than I knew myself, and He would do what was best for me and John."

A blessing was given, and weeks, months, and years passed by. John's cancer miraculously went into remission. He was able to complete his university studies and to obtain gainful employment. John and Heather continued to strengthen their relationship and enjoy life together.

Some time later I received a letter from John and Heather informing me that the cancer had returned. Chemotherapy was resumed and surgery scheduled. John explained: "Not only did this news come as a disappointment to Heather and me, but we were puzzled by it. Was there something we did not learn the first time? Did the Lord expect something more from us? Growing up as Latter-day Saints, it was common to go to church and hear the phrase, 'every trial God gives us is for our benefit.' Well, to be honest, I could not see how this was benefitting me!

"So I began to pray for clarity and for the Lord to help me understand why this recurrence of the cancer was happening. One day as I was reading in the New Testament I received my answer. I read the account of Christ and His Apostles on the sea when a tempest arose. Fearing the boat would capsize, the disciples went to the Savior and asked, 'Master, carest thou not that we perish?' This is exactly how I felt! Carest thou not that I have cancer? Carest thou not that we want to start a family? But as I read on in the story, I found my answer. The Lord looked at them and said, 'O ye of little faith,' and He stretched forth His hand and calmed the waters.

"In that moment I had to ask myself, 'Do I really believe this? Do I really believe He calmed the waters that day? Or is it just a nice story to read about?' The answer is: I do believe, and because I know He calmed the waters, I instantly knew He could heal me. Up until this point, I had a hard time reconciling the need for my faith in Christ with the inevitability of His will. I saw them as two separate things, and sometimes I felt that one contradicted the other. 'Why should I have faith if His will ultimately is what will prevail?' I asked. After this experience, I knew that having faith— at least in my circumstance—was not necessarily knowing that He *would* heal me, but that He *could* heal me. I had to believe that He could, and then whether it happened was up to Him.

"As I allowed those two ideas to coexist in my life, focused faith in Jesus Christ and complete submission to His will, I found greater comfort and peace. It has been so remarkable to see the Lord's hand in our lives. Things have fallen into place, miracles have happened, and we continually are humbled to see God's plan for us unfold."

I repeat for emphasis John's statement: "As I allowed those two ideas to coexist in my life, focused faith in Jesus Christ and complete submission to His will, I found greater comfort and peace."

Righteousness and faith certainly are instrumental in moving mountains—if moving mountains accomplishes God's purposes and is in accordance with His will. Righteousness and faith certainly are instrumental in healing the sick, deaf, or lame—if such healing accomplishes God's purposes and is in accordance with His will. Thus, even with our strong faith, many mountains will not be moved. And not all of the sick and infirm will be healed. If all opposition were curtailed, if all maladies were removed, then the primary purposes of the Father's plan would be frustrated.

Many of the lessons we are to learn in mortality can be received only through the things we experience and sometimes suffer. And God expects and trusts us to face temporary mortal adversity with His help so we can learn what we need to learn and ultimately become what we are to become in eternity.

This story about John and Heather is both ordinary and extraordinary. This young couple is representative of millions of faithful, covenant-keeping Latter-day Saints all over the world who are pressing forward along the strait and narrow path with steadfast faith in Christ and a perfect brightness of hope. John and Heather were not serving in highly visible leadership positions in the Church, they were not related to General Authorities, and sometimes they had doubts and fears. In many of these aspects, their story is quite ordinary.

But this young man and young woman were blessed in extraordinary ways to learn essential lessons for eternity through affliction and hardship. I have shared this episode with you because John and Heather, who are just like so many faithful people, came to understand that not shrinking is more important than surviving. Thus, their experience was not primarily about living and dying; rather, it was about learning, living, and becoming.

The potent spiritual combination of exercising faith in and on the holy name of Jesus Christ, of meekly submitting to His will and timing, of pressing forward "with unwearied diligence" (Helaman 15:6), and of acknowledging His hand in all things yields the peaceable things of the kingdom of God that bring joy and eternal life (see Doctrine and Covenants 42:61). As this couple faced seemingly overwhelming challenges, they lived a "peaceable life in all godliness and honesty" (1 Timothy 2:2). They walked peaceably (see Moroni 7:4) with and among the children of men. "And the peace of God, which passeth all understanding, [kept their] hearts and minds through Christ Jesus" (Philippians 4:7).

Perhaps their story is, has been, or could be your story. You are facing, have faced, or will yet face equivalent challenges in your life with the same courage, spiritual perspective, and personal peace that John and Heather did. I do not know why some people learn the lessons of eternity through trial and suffering, while others learn similar lessons through rescue and healing. I do not know all of the reasons, all of the purposes, and I do not know everything about the Lord's timing. With Nephi, you and I can say that we "do not know the meaning of all things" (1 Nephi 11:17).

But some things I absolutely do know. I know we are spirit sons and daughters of a loving Heavenly Father. I know the Eternal Father is the author of the plan of happiness. I know Jesus Christ is our Savior and Redeemer. I know Jesus enabled the Father's plan through His infinite and eternal Atonement. I know that the Lord, who was "bruised, broken, [and] torn for us" ("Jesus of Nazareth, Savior and King," *Hymns,* no. 181*),* can succor and strengthen "his people according to their infirmities" (Alma 7:12). And I know some of the greatest blessings of mortality are to not shrink, to allow our individual will to be "swallowed up in the will of the Father" (Mosiah 15:7), and to receive "peace of conscience" (Mosiah 4:3).

Though I do not know everything about how and when and where and why these blessings occur, I do know and I witness they are real. I testify that all of these things are true—and that we know enough by the power of the Holy Ghost to bear sure witness of their divinity, reality, and efficacy.

SUMMARY

Paul taught, "For the kingdom of God is not meat and drink; but righteousness, and peace, and joy in the Holy Ghost. . . . Let us therefore follow after the things which make for peace" (Romans 14:17, 19). And Peter declared, "For he that will love life, and see good days, let him refrain his tongue from evil, and his lips that they speak no guile: Let him eschew evil, and do good; let him seek peace, and ensue it" (1 Peter 3:10–11).

Every human soul yearns for peace—even peace of conscience and the peace that passeth all understanding. This blessing is not obtained with worldly wealth or through professional accomplishment, personal prominence, prestige, or power. The Lord Jesus Christ is the only source of enduring personal peace. Faith and hope in Him, obedience to His commandments, and pressing forward valiantly in the journey of mortality invite the spiritual gift of peace into our lives. And His peace fortifies us to face adversity with assurance and perspective—and helps us to "continue in the faith grounded and settled, and be not moved away from the hope of the gospel" (Colossians 1:23).

> *Where can I turn for peace?*
> *Where is my solace*
> *When other sources cease to make me whole?*
> *When with a wounded heart, anger, or malice,*
> *I draw myself apart,*
> *Searching my soul?*
>
> *Where, when my aching grows,*
> *Where, when I languish,*
> *Where, in my need to know, where can I run?*
> *Where is the quiet hand to calm my anguish?*
> *Who, who can understand?*
> *He, only One.*
>
> *He answers privately,*
> *Reaches my reaching*

In my Gethsemane, Savior and Friend.
Gentle the peace he finds for my beseeching.
Constant he is and kind,
Love without end.
("Where Can I Turn for Peace?" Hymns, *no. 129)*

Related Readings

1. Richard G. Scott, "Peace of Conscience and Peace of Mind," *Ensign,* November 2004, 15–18.

2. Richard G. Scott, "The Path to Peace and Joy," *Ensign,* November 2000, 25–27.

3. Henry B. Eyring, "A Life Founded in Light and Truth," BYU Devotional, August 15, 2000. Available online at speeches .byu.edu.

4. Jeffrey R. Holland, "'The Peaceable Things of the Kingdom,'" *Ensign,* November 1996, 82–84.

5. Thomas S. Monson, "The Path to Peace," *Ensign,* May 1994, 60–63.

6. Sheri L. Dew, "Our Only Chance," *Ensign,* May 1999, 66–67.

Explore these concepts further with a group discussion.

Scan this code or visit
seek.deseretbook.com/powertobecome

CONSIDER

What can and should I do in my life to appropriately seek for "the peace which passeth all understanding"?

Consider

What am I learning about the Savior as the "Prince of Peace" (Isaiah 9:6)?

CONSIDER

How does learning about and understanding the relationship between adversity and personal peace impact my discipleship?

My Own Questions to Consider

SCRIPTURES RELATED TO WHAT I AM LEARNING

AN INVITATION TO LEARN, TO ACT, AND TO BECOME		
What additional doctrines and principles, if understood, would help me appropriately invite peace of conscience into my life?	What can and should I do to act in those doctrines and principles?	How will I know if I am making progress in striving to become more like the Savior?

AN INVITATION TO LEARN, TO ACT, AND TO BECOME		
What additional doctrines and principles, if understood, would help me appropriately invite peace of conscience into my life?	What can and should I do to act in those doctrines and principles?	How will I know if I am making progress in striving to become more like the Savior?

An Invitation to Learn, to Act, and to Become

What additional doctrines and principles, if understood, would help me appropriately invite peace of conscience into my life?	What can and should I do to act in those doctrines and principles?	How will I know if I am making progress in striving to become more like the Savior?

CHAPTER 3

POWER TO BECOME, PRIESTHOOD ORDINANCES, AND WILLING OBEDIENCE

For mortal men and women, the power to become is possible because of and through the Atonement of Jesus Christ. "We believe that through the Atonement of Christ, all mankind may be saved, by obedience to the laws and ordinances of the Gospel" (Articles of Faith 1:3).

Priesthood ordinances and willing obedience are essential as we press forward along the pathway to perfection in the journey of mortality.

Ordinances performed by proper priesthood authority and received worthily provide access to all of the blessings made possible through the Savior's atoning sacrifice. "We believe that the first principles and ordinances of the Gospel are: first, Faith in the Lord Jesus Christ; second, Repentance; third, Baptism by immersion for the remission of sins; fourth, Laying on of hands for the gift of the Holy Ghost" (Articles of Faith 1:4). Without the blessings and gifts of the Atonement received through priesthood ordinances, our progress in mortality and eternity would be thwarted.

"And this shall be our covenant—that we will walk in all the ordinances of the Lord" (Doctrine and Covenants 136:4).

"Wherefore he that prayeth, whose spirit is contrite, the same is accepted of me if he obey mine ordinances.

"He that speaketh, whose spirit is contrite, whose language is meek and edifieth, the same is of God if he obey mine ordinances" (Doctrine and Covenants 52:15–16).

Obedience fuels faith in the Lord and reflects the sincerity and intensity of our ongoing turn from self to the Savior.

"The Spirit of truth is of God. I am the Spirit of truth, and John bore record of me, saying: He received a fulness of truth, yea, even of all truth;

"And no man receiveth a fulness unless he keepeth his commandments.

"He that keepeth his commandments receiveth truth and light, until he is glorified in truth and knoweth all things" (Doctrine and Covenants 93:26–28).

"And again I say unto you, if ye observe to do whatsoever I command you, I, the Lord, will turn away all wrath and indignation from you, and the gates of hell shall not prevail against you" (Doctrine and Covenants 98:22).

"And in nothing doth man offend God, or against none is his wrath kindled, save those who confess not his hand in all things, and obey not his commandments" (Doctrine and Covenants 59:21).

"Hath the Lord as great delight in burnt offerings and sacrifices, as in obeying the voice of the Lord? Behold, to obey is better than sacrifice, and to hearken than the fat of rams" (1 Samuel 15:22).

"If ye love me, keep my commandments" (John 14:15).

"Behold, this is your work, to keep my commandments, yea, with all your might, mind and strength" (Doctrine and Covenants 11:20).

The Power of Godliness

An ordinance is a sacred, formal act performed by the authority of the priesthood. Some ordinances are essential to our exaltation; these are called saving ordinances. They include baptism (see Matthew 3:16; Doctrine and Covenants 20:72–74), confirmation (see Doctrine and Covenants 20:68; 33:15), ordination to the Melchizedek Priesthood for men (see Doctrine and Covenants 84:6–16; 107:41–52), the temple endowment (see Doctrine and Covenants 124:39), and the marriage sealing (see Doctrine and Covenants 132:19–20). With each of these ordinances, we enter into solemn covenants with the Lord.

Ordinances help us learn and remember who we are as children of God; they also remind us of our spiritual responsibilities and duties. The Lord has provided ordinances to help us come unto Him and receive eternal life. As we honor ordinances, He strengthens us.

Priesthood ordinances open the door and provide access to the power of godliness.

"And this greater priesthood administereth the gospel and holdeth the key of the mysteries of the kingdom, even the key of the knowledge of God.

"Therefore, in the ordinances thereof, the power of godliness is manifest.

"And without the ordinances thereof, and the authority of the priesthood, the power of godliness is not manifest unto men in the flesh" (Doctrine and Covenants 84:19–21).

The human mind and mortal languages simply cannot define accurately or adequately the meaning of the scriptural phrase, "the power of godliness." But the totality of the blessings of the Atonement—redemption from sin; strength to do and to become good; the spiritual gift of personal peace; the compensating capacities that help us face disappointment, injustice, unfairness, inequity, and so much more—certainly constitute at least a portion of the power of godliness.

Lehi's vision provides an inspiring example of the relationship between the Savior's Atonement and priesthood ordinances. The central feature in Lehi's dream is the tree of life, a representation of "the love of God" (1 Nephi 11:21–22).

"For God so loved the world, that he gave his only begotten Son, that whosoever believeth in him should not perish, but have everlasting life" (John 3:16).

The birth, life, and atoning sacrifice of the Lord Jesus Christ are the greatest manifestations of God's love for His children. As Nephi testified, this love was "most desirable above all things" and "most joyous to the soul" (1 Nephi 11:22–23; see also 1 Nephi 8:12, 15). Chapter 11 of 1 Nephi presents a detailed description of the tree of life as a symbol for the life, ministry, and sacrifice of the Savior—the "condescension of God" (1 Nephi 11:16). The tree can be considered as a representation of Christ.

One way of thinking about the fruit on the tree is as a symbol for the blessings of the Atonement. Interestingly, an individual can obtain the path that leads to the tree only by entering through the gate—even the ordinances of baptism and confirmation. "For the gate by which ye should enter is repentance and baptism by water; and then cometh a remission of your sins by fire and by the Holy Ghost" (2 Nephi 31:17). Pressing forward to and partaking of the fruit of the tree may represent the receiving of additional ordinances and covenants whereby the Atonement can become fully efficacious in our lives. The fruit is described as "desirable to make one happy" (1 Nephi 8:10) and produces great joy and the desire to share that joy with others.

Please now consider the sobering significance of the implications that arise from Lehi's vision and the verses previously referred to from section 84 of the Doctrine and Covenants. To come unto the Savior, an individual *must* first pass through the gate of baptism and receive the gift of the Holy Ghost—and then continue to press forward along the path of covenants and ordinances that leads to the Savior and the blessings of His Atonement (see 2 Nephi 31). Priesthood ordinances are essential to fully "come unto Christ, and be perfected in him" (Moroni 10:32; see also vv. 30–33). Without the ordinances, an individual cannot receive all of the blessings made possible through the Lord's infinite and eternal atoning sacrifice (see Alma 34:10–14)—even the power of godliness.

President Boyd K. Packer declared: "The mariner gets his bearing from light coming from celestial bodies—the sun by day, the stars by night. . . .

"The spiritual sextant, which each of us has, also functions on the principle of light from celestial sources. Set that sextant in your mind to the word *covenant* or the word *ordinance*. The light will come through. Then you can fix your position and set a true course in life.

"No matter what citizenship or race, whether male or female, no matter what occupation, no matter your education, regardless of the generation in which one lives, life is a homeward journey for all of us, back to the presence of God in his celestial kingdom.

"Ordinances and covenants become our credentials for admission into His presence. To worthily receive them is the quest of a lifetime; to keep them thereafter is the challenge of mortality.

"Once we have received them for ourselves and for our families, we are obligated to provide these ordinances vicariously for our kindred dead, indeed for the whole human family" ("Covenants," 24).

A person exercises moral agency and decides if he or she will receive the ordinances of the restored gospel. However, that individual does not and cannot determine the consequences for electing to forgo these sacred ordinances. President James E. Faust taught, "Going to the temple is a matter of choice, but many do not realize that in order to come unto Christ receiving the ordinances of the temple is not optional, it is essential. No one will be able to come unto Christ without these steps and ordinances" (James P. Bell, *In the Strength of the Lord,* 443).

Truly, the power of godliness is manifest in the ordinances of the priesthood.

Priesthood Ordinances and Hearts

At a solemn assembly held in the Kirtland Temple on April 6, 1837, the Prophet Joseph Smith spoke on matters pertaining to the priesthood and priesthood quorums. He explained to the assembled brethren:

"After all that has been said, the greatest and most important duty is to preach the Gospel" (*History of the Church,* 2:478).

Almost precisely seven years later, on April 7, 1844, Joseph Smith delivered a sermon now known as the King Follett discourse. In that address the Prophet Joseph Smith declared:

"The greatest responsibility in this world that God has laid upon us is to seek after our dead. The apostle says, 'They without us cannot be made perfect;' for it is necessary that the sealing power should be in our hands to seal our children and our dead for the fulness of the dispensation of times—a dispensation to meet the promises made by Jesus Christ before the foundation of the world for the salvation of man" (*History of the Church,* 6:313).

Some individuals may wonder how both preaching the gospel *and* seeking after our dead can be simultaneously the greatest duty and responsibility God has placed upon His children. But these teachings of the Prophet highlight the unity and oneness of the latter-day work of salvation. Missionary work and family history and temple work are complementary and interrelated aspects of one great work, "that in the dispensation of the fulness of times he might gather together in one all things in Christ, both which are in heaven, and which are on earth; even in him" (Ephesians 1:10).

Preaching the gospel and seeking after our dead are two divinely appointed responsibilities that relate both to our hearts and to priesthood ordinances. The essence of the Lord's work is changing, turning, and purifying hearts through covenants and ordinances performed by proper priesthood authority.

The word *heart* is used over a thousand times in the standard works and symbolizes the inner feelings of an individual. Thus, our hearts—the sum total of our desires, affections, intentions, motives, and attitudes—define who we are and determine what we will become.

The Lord's purpose for missionary work is to invite all to come unto Christ, receive the ordinances, covenants, and blessings of the restored gospel, and endure to the end through faith in Christ (see *Preach My Gospel,* 1). We do not share the gospel merely to increase the numerical size and strength of the latter-day Church.

Rather, we seek to fulfill the divinely appointed responsibility to proclaim the reality of the Father's plan of happiness, the divinity of His Only Begotten Son, Jesus Christ, and the efficacy of the Savior's atoning sacrifice. Inviting all to "come unto Christ" (Moroni 10:30–33), experiencing the "mighty change of heart" (Alma 5:12–14), and offering the ordinances of salvation to individuals in mortality not yet under covenant are the fundamental objectives of preaching the gospel.

Enabling the exaltation of the living and the dead is the Lord's purpose for our building temples and performing vicarious ordinances. We do not worship in holy temples solely to have a memorable individual or family experience. Rather, we seek to fulfill the divinely appointed responsibility to offer the ordinances of salvation and exaltation to the entire human family. Planting in the hearts of the children the promises made to the fathers—even Abraham, Isaac, and Jacob—turning the hearts of the children to their own fathers, and performing family history research and vicarious ordinances in the temple are labors that bless individuals in the spirit world not yet under covenant.

The Lord's work is one majestic work focused upon hearts, covenants, and priesthood ordinances. Perhaps the Lord was emphasizing this truth in the very sequence of events that occurred as the fulness of the gospel was restored to the earth in these latter days.

In the Sacred Grove, Joseph Smith saw and talked with the Eternal Father and Jesus Christ. This vision ushered in the "dispensation of the fulness of times" (Ephesians 1:10) and enabled Joseph to learn about the true nature of the Godhead and of continual revelation.

Approximately three years later, in response to earnest prayer on the evening of September 21, 1823, Joseph's bedroom filled with light until it was "lighter than at noonday" (Joseph

Smith–History 1:30). A personage appeared at his bedside, called the young boy by name, and declared "he was a messenger sent from the presence of God . . . and that his name was Moroni" (v. 33). He instructed Joseph about the coming forth of the Book of Mormon. And then Moroni quoted from the book of Malachi in the Old Testament, with a little variation from the language used in the King James Version: "Behold, I will reveal unto you the Priesthood, by the hand of Elijah the prophet, before the coming of the great and dreadful day of the Lord. . . . And he shall plant in the hearts of the children the promises made to the fathers, and the hearts of the children shall turn to their fathers. If it were not so, the whole earth would be utterly wasted at his coming" (Joseph Smith–History 1:38–39).

Moroni's instructions to the young prophet ultimately included two primary themes: (1) the Book of Mormon, and (2) the words of Malachi foretelling the role of Elijah in the restoration "of all things, which God hath spoken by the mouth of all his holy prophets since the world began" (Acts 3:21). Thus, the introductory events of the Restoration revealed a correct understanding of the Godhead, established the reality of continuing revelation, emphasized the importance of the Book of Mormon, and anticipated the work of salvation and exaltation for both the living and the dead.

Please now consider the role of the Book of Mormon in changing hearts and of the spirit of Elijah in turning hearts preparatory to worthily receiving priesthood ordinances.

The Book of Mormon in combination with the Spirit of the Lord is the greatest single tool God has given us to convert the world (see Ezra Taft Benson, "A New Witness for Christ," 7). This Restoration volume of scripture is the keystone of our religion and is essential in bringing souls to the Savior. The Book of Mormon is another testament of Jesus Christ—a vital confirming witness of the divinity of the Redeemer in a world that grows ever more secular and cynical. Hearts are changed as individuals read and study the Book of Mormon and pray with real intent to learn of the truthfulness of the book.

The spirit of Elijah is "a manifestation of the Holy Ghost bearing witness of the divine nature of the family" (Russell M. Nelson, "A New Harvest Time," 34). This distinctive influence of the Holy Ghost bears powerful witness of the Father's plan of happiness and draws people to search out and cherish their ancestors and family members—both past and present. The spirit of Elijah affects people both inside and outside of the Church and causes hearts to turn to the fathers.

The Lord's work is one majestic work focused upon hearts that change and turn, upon sacred covenants, and upon the power of godliness manifested through priesthood ordinances.

The Lord declared, "I am able to do mine own work" (2 Nephi 27:21), and "I will hasten my work in its time" (Doctrine and Covenants 88:73). Today we are witnesses of His hastening of His work.

We live, learn, and serve in the dispensation of the fulness of times. It was necessary in this final dispensation "that a whole and complete and perfect union, and welding together of dispensations, and keys, and powers, and glories should take place, and be revealed from the days of Adam even to the present time. And not only this, but those things which never have been revealed from the foundation of the world, but have been kept hid from the wise and prudent, shall be revealed . . . in this, the dispensation of the fulness of times" (Doctrine and Covenants 128:18). The Prophet Joseph explained, "All the *ordinances* and duties that ever have been required by the Priesthood, under the directions and commandments of the Almighty in any of the dispensations, shall all be had in the last dispensation . . . bringing to pass the restoration spoken of by the mouth of all the Holy Prophets" (*History of the Church,* 4:210–11; emphasis added).

Joseph further proclaimed that preparatory to the Second Coming of the Lord Jesus Christ, "the dispensation of the fullness of times will bring to light the things that have been revealed in all former dispensations; also other things that have not been before revealed" (*History of the Church,* 4:426). As the Apostle Paul declared, "In the dispensation of the fulness of times [God will] gather together in one all things in Christ, both which are in heaven, and which are on earth; even in him" (Ephesians 1:10). Thus, the overarching purpose of this concluding dispensation is to gather together in one all things in Christ. And access to the power of godliness through priesthood ordinances will be greater in this dispensation than at any previous time in the history of the earth.

Recognizing the eternal importance of the distinctive dispensation in which we live should influence all that we do and strive to become. The work of salvation to be accomplished in these last days is grand, vast, essential, and urgent. How grateful each of us should be for the blessings and responsibilities of living in this specific season of the final dispensation. How humble we should be knowing that "of him unto whom much is given much is required" (Doctrine and Covenants 82:3).

WILLING OBEDIENCE

The first law of heaven is obedience.

"Hearken, O ye elders of my church, who have assembled yourselves together in my name, even Jesus Christ the Son of the living God, the Savior of the world; inasmuch as ye believe on my name and keep my commandments.

"Again I say unto you, *hearken* and *hear* and *obey* the law which I shall give unto you" (Doctrine and Covenants 42:1–2; emphasis added).

Please notice how the word *obey* is linked to both *hearing* and *hearkening*. Hearing is the process of giving an ear to, and hearkening connotes applying the mind to what one hears. Obeying, then, results from hearing the word of God (see Romans 10:17; Alma 32) and pondering (see 1 Nephi 11:1; Moroni 10:3) and studying it out in our own minds (see Doctrine and Covenants 9:8).

Obedience is aligning our individual will with God's will. "God's blessings . . . come by unforced obedience to the laws upon which they are predicated (see D&C 130:20–21). Thus our deepest desires determine our degree of 'obedience to the unenforceable'" (Neal A. Maxwell, "'Swallowed Up in the Will of the Father,'" 24).

"And there stood one among them that was like unto God, and he said unto those who were with him: We will go down, for there is space there, and we will take of these materials, and we will make an earth whereon these may dwell;

"And we will prove them herewith, to see if they will do all things whatsoever the Lord their God shall command them;

"And they who keep their first estate shall be added upon; and they who keep not their first estate shall not have glory in the same kingdom with those who keep their first estate; and they who keep their second estate shall have glory added upon their heads for ever and ever" (Abraham 3:24–26).

"There is a law, irrevocably decreed in heaven before the foundations of this world, upon which all blessings are predicated—

"And when we obtain any blessing from God, it is by obedience to that law upon which it is predicated" (Doctrine and Covenants 130:20–21).

"For behold, I reveal unto you a new and an everlasting covenant; and if ye abide not that covenant, then are ye damned; for no one can reject this covenant and be permitted to enter into my glory.

"For all who will have a blessing at my hands shall abide the law which was appointed for that blessing, and the conditions thereof, as were instituted from before the foundation of the world" (Doctrine and Covenants 132:4–5).

"And in nothing doth man offend God, or against none is his wrath kindled, save those who confess not his hand in all things, and obey not his commandments" (Doctrine and Covenants 59:21).

"Behold, the Lord requireth the heart and a willing mind; and the willing and obedient shall eat the good of the land of Zion in these last days.

"And the rebellious shall be cut off out of the land of Zion, and shall be sent away, and shall not inherit the land.

"For, verily I say that the rebellious are not of the blood of Ephraim, wherefore they shall be plucked out" (Doctrine and Covenants 64:34–36).

The Savior's pathway to perfection was marked by complete and willing obedience and submission to the will of His Father.

"I came down from heaven, not to do mine own will, but the will of him that sent me" (John 6:38).

"Though he were a Son, yet learned he obedience by the things which he suffered;

"And being made perfect, he became the author of eternal salvation unto all them that obey him" (Hebrews 5:8–9).

The Lord's life was devoted totally to obeying His Father.

Obedience operates at a number of different levels. Elder Bruce R. McConkie explained, "*Obedience* is the first law of heaven, the cornerstone upon which all righteousness and progression rest. It consists in *compliance* with divine law, in *conformity* to the mind and will of Deity, in complete *subjection* to God and his commands. To obey gospel law is to yield obedience to the Lord, to execute the commands of and be ruled by him whose we are" (*Mormon Doctrine,* 539; emphasis added).

Note how Elder McConkie included the elements of *compliance, conformity,* and *subjection* or *submission* in his description of obedience. Each of these three elements can be considered as a progressive level of obedience. Thus, obedience is not simply a passive steady state; rather, obedience grows, develops, deepens, and expands as we press forward with a steadfastness in Christ. Our experience with and understanding of the principle of obedience should change as we develop spiritually and as we gain additional light and knowledge—line upon line and precept upon precept. Also, our spiritual expectations should increase and intensify as we continue to faithfully obey God's commandments.

A series of comparisons illustrates how obedience operates at different levels.

It is one thing to obey in order to qualify for and *receive blessings;* it is quite another thing to obey as a preparation to *give* and to *serve more effectively.*

It is one thing to merely and perhaps mechanically *comply*

with God's commandments; it is quite another thing to obey and thereby fully *submit* and subject oneself to the will and timetable of the Lord.

It is a good thing to obey out of a sense of *duty;* but it is an even greater thing, a more spiritually demanding thing, to obey through *love.*

It is one thing to reluctantly or grudgingly *conform* to commandments; it is a different thing to joyfully "obey and observe to perform every word of command with *exactness*" (Alma 57:21; emphasis added) and to cheerfully "*observe strictly* to keep the commandments of God" (Helaman 13:1; emphasis added).

It is one thing to perform the *outward actions* of obedience; it is quite a different thing to *become inwardly* what the commandments are intended to help us become.

It is one thing to obey the *institutional, public,* and *shared* commandments associated with the Lord's kingdom on earth—commandments such as the law of chastity, the law of tithing, and the Word of Wisdom; it is an even greater thing to receive and respond to the *individual, private,* and *personally revealed* commandments that result from continual and faithful obedience.

Ultimately, we obey willingly because we love the Lord and are striving to obtain the blessings and power to become more like Him.

Commandments Not a Few

"Yea, blessed are they whose feet stand upon the land of Zion, who have obeyed my gospel; for they shall receive for their reward *the good things of the earth,* and it shall bring forth in its strength.

"And they shall also be crowned with *blessings from above,* yea, and with *commandments not a few,* and with *revelations in their time*—they that are faithful and diligent before me" (Doctrine and Covenants 59:3–4; emphasis added).

We learn in these verses that those who obey the gospel shall receive the good things of the earth, blessings from above, commandments not a few, and revelations in their time. In particular I want to draw attention to the phrase "and with commandments not a few."

I have attempted to differentiate between obedience that is predominantly complying and conforming in nature and a higher level of obedience that includes spiritual submission and enables us to receive "commandments not a few." Obedience that is primarily complying and conforming is good. But a higher level of obedience that stretches beyond the letter of the law and to the spirit of the law is both heartfelt and willing—and it brings individualized gospel insight, perspective, and power that are precious beyond measure.

As described in the Doctrine and Covenants:

"Behold, the Lord requireth the *heart* and a willing mind; and the *willing* and *obedient* shall eat the good of the land of Zion in these last days" (Doctrine and Covenants 64:34; emphasis added).

"But unto him that keepeth my commandments I will give the mysteries of my kingdom, and the same shall be in him a well of living water, springing up unto everlasting life" (Doctrine and Covenants 63:23).

Progressing from the level of complying obedience to the level of heartfelt and willing obedience does not occur quickly or all at once. Nor is it merely a matter of greater personal discipline; it is a change of disposition, a change of heart. And this gradual change of heart is one that the Lord accomplishes within us, through the power of His Spirit, in a line-upon-line fashion.

For example, in Philippians 2:12, Paul encourages the Saints to "work out [their] own salvation with fear and trembling." But how are we to do that? Note the answer that follows in verse 13: "For it is God which worketh in you both to will and to do of his good pleasure." That is, we give ourselves to the Lord and choose to be changed. He is working on us and in us. It is vitally important for all of us to remember that progressing to higher and more spiritually demanding levels of obedience is not simply a matter of more personal determination, more grit, and more willpower; rather, it is accomplished through the enabling power of the Atonement of the Lord Jesus Christ.

Closely associated with obeying with a willing heart is reaching a point where we no longer are driven or directed by *rules;* instead, we learn to govern our lives by *principle.* To be sure, we keep the rules, but we also begin to ask ourselves, "What is the principle involved here?" Such a person becomes less dependent upon external scaffolding and structure and more dependent upon quiet and ongoing divine direction. As the Prophet Joseph explained, "I teach them correct principles, and they govern themselves" (*The Teachings of Joseph Smith,* 32).

The pathway to perfection in our mortal journey takes us to and through "letter of the law" obedience to public and institutional commandments and onward to a spirit of devoted discipleship and a private, personal, and individual change of heart.

President Ezra Taft Benson emphasized the difference between reluctant obedience and willing obedience: "When obedience ceases to be an irritant and becomes our quest, in that moment God will endow us with power" (in Donald L. Staheli, "Obedience—Life's Greatest Challenge," 82).

I find it fascinating that one of the greatest blessings related to keeping God's commandments is additional commandments. Now, individuals who find commandments restrictive and constraining clearly will not regard more commandments as a blessing. But the Apostle John taught that for one who has come unto Christ and been born again, God's "commandments are not grievous" (1 John 5:3). Thus, individuals who have eyes to see and ears to hear will readily recognize the consummate spiritual benefit that comes from extra direction from heaven. What are these "commandments not a few," and how do we receive them?

The individual and personal "commandments not a few" we receive frequently tend to focus upon good things we can and should do to develop and deepen our discipleship—as opposed to focusing primarily upon the bad things we must avoid or overcome. Such instructions typically are proactive and anticipatory in nature. Consider, for example, the teachings of President Spencer W. Kimball concerning fast offerings. He stated: "I think that when we are affluent, as many of us are, that we ought to be very, very generous. . . . I think we should be very generous and give, instead of the amount we saved by our two meals of fasting, perhaps much, much more—ten times more where we are in a position to do it" (in Conference Report, April 1974, 184).

Thus, an individual or a family may be prompted to freely and willingly and cheerfully contribute to the fast-offering fund at a level far beyond the routine and basic "letter of the law" standards with which most of us are familiar. The commandment "not a few" in this example is gladly obeyed in order to bless and strengthen others who have serious challenges and insufficient resources.

Consider the example of living "commandments not a few" evident in the story of one family. Albert Frehner and Matilda Reber were married on April 20, 1888, in the St. George Temple.

Albert and Matilda then established their humble home in Littlefield, Arizona. To provide for their family, Brother Frehner hauled freight between El Dorado Canyon and Bonelli's Ferry. Sister Frehner nurtured their growing family and took care of the household chores such as cleaning, making soap, canning and drying vegetables and fruit, knitting socks and sweaters, and sewing all other needed clothing. For these stalwart Saints it was a hard and a happy life together in an arid and desolate place.

Albert and Matilda had been married for ten years when Brother Frehner was called in 1898 by President Lorenzo Snow to serve as a missionary in Switzerland, his native land. At the time Albert received the call to serve, Matilda was expecting their fifth child. However, it never entered their hearts or minds to refuse the call, and both gladly accepted the challenge. Matilda assumed the total responsibility for the care of their young family, for their cotton farm, and for running the post office out of a small room in her home. She also boarded the local schoolteacher. Five months after Albert left on his mission, Matilda gave birth to twin girls, Edith and Ethel.

I have provided this background information about Matilda and her circumstances as a context for the following incident. One day Sister Frehner was attending to her duties in the post office. A man, as he was ready to depart after completing his postal business, gave Matilda twenty-five cents to send to Albert in the mission field. Twenty-five cents does not sound like much to you and to me today, but to Matilda it meant a great deal! Sister Frehner thanked the good brother and then asked him if she could use two cents of the money to buy a stamp. Matilda explained that she had written a letter to Albert a week or two earlier but did not have the two cents to purchase the necessary postage. The man readily agreed to her proposal, the stamp was procured, and the letter was mailed.

Please consider that Matilda was the manager of the post office. She easily could have borrowed and used a stamp—fully intending to repay the two cents when she was in a position to do so. And no one would have known. In her dire financial situation, it certainly would have seemed reasonable to go ahead and mail her letter at the time she wrote it. No one would have known!

But Matilda was obedient to a personal commandment "not a few" related to her honesty and integrity. And Sister Frehner simply refused to use, in any way, something for which she could not pay. She also was careful to seek the man's permission to use a portion of the money for a purpose other than that which he had intended. The example of Matilda, my great-grandmother, has had a profound and lasting impact upon my life. Sister Frehner is an example of a devoted disciple and of integrity and honesty with God, of integrity and honesty with herself, and of integrity and honesty with other people.

A few additional examples may be helpful. Please keep in mind, however, that I am not attempting to provide a prescriptive and comprehensive list of what "commandments not a few" are or should be. Such commandments are individual and quite personal; nonetheless, additional illustrations can help us to better comprehend this principle.

We may receive "commandments not a few" and "revelations in their time" about appropriate ways to improve our patterns of worship—both at home and at church.

A home or visiting teacher may receive "commandments not a few" and "revelations in their time" about ministering to the needs of specific individuals and focusing less upon merely making visits and presenting prepared messages.

We may receive "commandments not a few" and "revelations in their time" about the importance of and reverence for our physical bodies as a key element in the Father's plan of happiness. "Know ye not that ye are the temple of God, and that the Spirit of God dwelleth in you?" (1 Corinthians 3:16).

A husband or wife may receive "commandments not a few" and "revelations in their time" about communicating with and supporting a spouse who has received a new calling at church or who may feel overwhelmed and inadequate at home or at work.

We may receive "commandments not a few" and "revelations in their time" about appropriate ways to use various technologies to invite the constant companionship of the Holy Ghost—and to enlarge our capacity to live, to love, and to serve in meaningful ways.

A child may receive "commandments not a few" and "revelations in their time" about constructive ways of overcoming contention with siblings and becoming a peacemaker in the home.

We may receive "commandments not a few" and "revelations in their time" about living a virtuous, chaste, and pure life in a world that grows ever more coarse and impure.

We may receive "commandments not a few" and "revelations in their time" about preparing effectively to participate in frequently repeated priesthood ordinances such as the sacrament and vicarious temple ordinances.

As disciples pressing forward on the pathway to perfection, we may receive "commandments not a few" and "revelations in their time" about striving to "have no more disposition to do evil, but to do good continually" (Mosiah 5:2).

We may receive "commandments not a few" and "revelations in their time" about moving beyond merely dressing modestly to becoming an authentically and consistently modest person in mind, heart, and behavior.

We may receive "commandments not a few" and "revelations in their time" about ways to improve our personal and private religious behavior such as scripture study, prayer, and fasting.

We may receive "commandments not a few" and "revelations in their time" about the spiritual gift of discernment and becoming "quick to observe" (Mormon 1:2) in our homes, in our Church service, and in all other aspects of our lives.

"Commandments not a few" are not oppressive but liberating, not dour but joyful, and not forbidding but enlivening.

"And moreover, I would desire that ye should consider on the blessed and happy state of those that keep the commandments of God. For behold, they are blessed in all things, both temporal and spiritual; and if they hold out faithful to the end they are received into heaven, that thereby they may dwell with God in a state of never-ending happiness. O remember, remember that these things are true; for the Lord God hath spoken it" (Mosiah 2:41).

Such divine instructions also provide a periodic update on the progress we are making in the journey of mortality.

"And if your eye be single to my glory, your whole bodies shall be filled with light, and there shall be no darkness in you; and that body which is filled with light comprehendeth all things" (Doctrine and Covenants 88:67).

"All kingdoms have a law given;

"And there are many kingdoms; for there is no space in the which there is no kingdom; and there is no kingdom in which there is no space, either a greater or a lesser kingdom.

"And unto every kingdom is given a law; and unto every law there are certain bounds also and conditions.

"All beings who abide not in those conditions are not justified.

"For intelligence cleaveth unto intelligence; wisdom receiveth wisdom; truth embraceth truth; virtue loveth virtue; light cleaveth unto light; mercy hath compassion on mercy and claimeth her own; justice continueth its course and claimeth its own; judgment goeth before the face of him who sitteth upon the throne and governeth and executeth all things" (Doctrine and Covenants 88:36–40).

The Home Is the Best Place to Experience Willing Obedience

The first, foremost, and greatest responsibility to teach and model obedience rests upon parents. We learn best to obey and to become from dear loved ones in a spiritually protected, safe, and secure home.

We are all familiar with Nephi's introductory comment in the Book of Mormon about "having been born of goodly parents, therefore I was taught somewhat in *all* the learning of my father" (1 Nephi 1:1; emphasis added). Clearly, the seeds of Nephi's consistent faithfulness and willing obedience were planted in the fertile soil of his soul and cultivated and nurtured in a gospel-centered home. It is significant that the final words Nephi recorded in his account reflect both his life's experience and the powerful influence of his home: "For what I seal on earth, shall be brought against you at the judgment bar; for thus hath the Lord commanded me, and *I must obey.* Amen" (2 Nephi 33:15; emphasis added).

Just as Nephi's benedictory words provide great insight into his life, so we also learn much about the Prophet Joseph Smith himself and about his home in a simple statement found in the Joseph Smith History. Recall that the young boy Joseph was visited and instructed three times during one night by Moroni. The day after the visitation, Joseph attempted to fulfill his regular responsibilities on the farm but was so exhausted he could not get anything done. Seeing the young boy's condition, Joseph's father instructed his son to return to their home. As Joseph was leaving the field and crossing the fence, he fell on the ground, and for a time he was quite unconscious of anything.

"The first thing that I can recollect was a voice speaking unto me, calling me by name. I looked up, and beheld the same messenger standing over my head, surrounded by light as before. He then again related unto me all that he had related to me the previous night, and commanded me to go to my father and tell him of the vision and commandments which I had received" (Joseph Smith–History 1:49).

At the beginning of verse 50 we find the simple two-word statement that tells us so much about Joseph and his home: "I obeyed." And Joseph's early experiences with heartfelt and willing obedience in his home provided a solid foundation upon which a lifetime of faithful and fearless leadership was built. As the Prophet Joseph explained, "I made this my rule: *When the Lord commands, do it*" (*History of the Church,* 2:170; emphasis in original).

It is not unrealistic to assert that in the times in which we live, parents in Zion must strive to create and maintain homes like Nephi's and Joseph's—homes in which parents and children alike learn about and gain experience with heartfelt and willing obedience. From such homes will come Latter-day Saints who are pure—certainly not perfect, but pure and without spot. And that purity produces a matchless power to learn, to act, to become, and to literally "chase darkness from among you" (Doctrine and Covenants 50:25). Personal purity brings forth unparalleled spiritual power, and our homes are the places in which heartfelt and willing obedience and personal purity bloom and blossom. Thus, a Christ-centered home is one of the most important settings for receiving and experiencing the power to become.

"Set in order [your] family, and see that they are more diligent and concerned at home, and pray always" (Doctrine and Covenants 93:50).

SUMMARY

Priesthood ordinances constitute the channel through which the power of godliness and the blessings of the Atonement of Jesus Christ can flow into our lives. An ordinance is a sacred physical act with symbolic meaning, such as baptism, confirmation, or the sacrament. The Lord's work is a labor of love focused upon hearts, covenants, and priesthood ordinances.

Obedience to gospel principles and ordinances frees a person from the spiritual bondage of sin (see John 8:31–36). As President Gordon B. Hinckley explained, "True freedom lies in obedience to the counsel of God. . . . The gospel is not a philosophy of repression, as so many regard it. It is a plan of freedom that gives discipline to appetite and direction to behavior" ("A Principle with a Promise," 521).

President Thomas S. Monson promised, "The knowledge which we seek, the answers for which we yearn, and the strength which we desire today to meet the challenges of a complex and changing world can be ours when we willingly obey the Lord's commandments" ("Obedience Brings Blessings," 92).

As we obtain a desire and determination to obey God's commandments with all of our hearts and with willing minds, we can qualify for and be blessed to receive "commandments not a few" and "revelations in their time." Such personal and private direction from our loving Heavenly Father is a supernal source of assurance, enlightenment, and joy.

The home is the ideal place for learning, teaching, and applying gospel principles. Latter-day prophets have urged families to give highest priority to family prayer, family home evening, gospel study and instruction, and wholesome family activities.

President David O. McKay succinctly summarized the role of priesthood ordinances and willing obedience upon the power to become. "What is the crowning glory of man in this earth so far as his individual achievement is concerned? It is character—character developed through obedience to the laws of life as revealed through the gospel of Jesus Christ, who came that we might have life and have it more abundantly [see John 10:10]. Man's chief concern in life should not be the acquiring of gold, or of fame, or of material possessions. It should not be the development of physical prowess, nor of intellectual strength, but his aim, the highest in life, should be the development of a Christ-like character" (*Teachings of Presidents of the Church: David O. McKay,* 220).

> *Keep the commandments; keep the commandments!*
> *In this there is safety; in this there is peace.*
> *He will send blessings; He will send blessings.*
> *Words of a prophet: Keep the commandments,*
> *In this there is safety and peace.*
> *("Keep the Commandments," Hymns, no. 303)*

Related Readings

1. Boyd K. Packer, "The Honor and Order of the Priesthood," *Ensign,* June 2012, 21–25.

2. D. Todd Christofferson, "The Power of Covenants," *Ensign,* May 2009, 19–23.

3. Dallin H. Oaks, "Good, Better, Best," *Ensign,* November 2007, 104–8.

4. Neal A. Maxwell, "The Pathway of Discipleship," BYU Fireside, January 4, 1998. Available online at speeches.byu .edu.

5. James E. Faust, "'The Great Imitator,'" *Ensign,* November 1987, 33–36.

6. Neal A. Maxwell, "Meekly Drenched in Destiny," BYU Fireside, September 5, 1982. Available online at speeches.byu .edu.

7. Bruce R. McConkie, "The Doctrine of the Priesthood," *Ensign,* May 1982, 32–34.

8. Boyd K. Packer, "Spiritual Crocodiles," *Ensign*, May 1976, 30–32.

9. J. Reuben Clark Jr., "The Priesthood," in Conference Report, April 1953, 52–56.

10. C. S. Lewis, *Mere Christianity.*

Explore these concepts further with a group discussion.

Scan this code or visit seek.deseretbook.com/powertobecome

CONSIDER

What can and should I do to receive more fully in my life "the power of godliness"?

CONSIDER

What am I learning about the role of priesthood ordinances in "[coming] unto Christ and [being] perfected in Him"?

CONSIDER

How should "commandments not a few" influence my discipleship?

MY OWN QUESTIONS TO CONSIDER

Scriptures Related to What I Am Learning

AN INVITATION TO LEARN, TO ACT, AND TO BECOME		
What additional doctrines and principles, if understood, would help me appropriately invite into my life the power of godliness through priesthood ordinances?	What can and should I do to act in those doctrines and principles?	How will I know if I am making progress in striving to become more like the Savior?

AN INVITATION TO LEARN, TO ACT, AND TO BECOME		
What additional doctrines and principles, if understood, would help me appropriately invite into my life the power of godliness through priesthood ordinances?	What can and should I do to act in those doctrines and principles?	How will I know if I am making progress in striving to become more like the Savior?

AN INVITATION TO LEARN, TO ACT, AND TO BECOME		
What additional doctrines and principles, if understood, would help me appropriately invite into my life the power of godliness through priesthood ordinances?	What can and should I do to act in those doctrines and principles?	How will I know if I am making progress in striving to become more like the Savior?

CHAPTER 4

Power to Become and Enduring Valiantly

In mortality we chart our course and begin to become what we ultimately will be in eternity. Our second estate (see Abraham 3:26) is not a probationary experience to be tolerated reluctantly and grudgingly. Rather, the scriptures indicate that we are to "*press forward* with a steadfastness in Christ, having a perfect brightness of hope, and a love of God and of all men. Wherefore, if ye shall press forward, feasting upon the word of Christ, and *endure to the end,* behold, thus saith the Father: Ye shall have eternal life" (2 Nephi 31:20; emphasis added).

"All thrones and dominions, principalities and powers, shall be revealed and set forth upon all who have *endured valiantly* for the gospel of Jesus Christ" (Doctrine and Covenants 121:29; emphasis added).

"My son, peace be unto thy soul; thine adversity and thine afflictions shall be but a small moment;

"And then, if thou *endure it well,* God shall exalt thee on high;

thou shalt triumph over all thy foes" (Doctrine and Covenants 121:7–8; emphasis added).

"And we know that all men must repent and believe on the name of Jesus Christ, and worship the Father in his name, and *endure in faith on his name to the end,* or they cannot be saved in the kingdom of God" (Doctrine and Covenants 20:29; emphasis added).

"And I heard a voice from the Father, saying: Yea, the words of my Beloved are true and faithful. He that *endureth to the end,* the same shall be saved.

"And now, my beloved brethren, I know by this that unless a man shall *endure to the end, in following the example of the Son of the living God,* he cannot be saved" (2 Nephi 31:15–16; emphasis added).

"I say unto you, if ye have come to a knowledge of the goodness of God, and his matchless power, and his wisdom, and his patience, and his long-suffering towards the children of men; and also, the atonement which has been prepared from the foundation of the world, that thereby salvation might come to him that should put his trust in the Lord, and should be diligent in keeping his commandments, and *continue in the faith even unto the end of his life,* I mean the life of the mortal body—

"I say, that this is the man who receiveth salvation, through the atonement which was prepared from the foundation of the world for all mankind, which ever were since the fall of Adam, or who are, or who ever shall be, even unto the end of the world" (Mosiah 4:6–7; emphasis added).

"But this much I can tell you, that if ye do not watch your-selves, and your thoughts, and your words, and your deeds, and observe the commandments of God, and *continue in the faith of what ye have heard concerning the coming of our Lord, even unto the end of your lives,* ye must perish. And now, O man, remember, and perish not" (Mosiah 4:30; emphasis added).

"Nevertheless, he that *endureth in faith* and doeth my will, the same shall overcome, and shall receive an inheritance upon the earth when the day of transfiguration shall come" (Doctrine and Covenants 63:20; emphasis added).

"*Continue in these things even unto the end,* and you shall have a crown of eternal life at the right hand of my Father, who is full of grace and truth" (Doctrine and Covenants 66:12; emphasis added).

"Seek to bring forth and establish my Zion. Keep my com-mandments in all things.

"And, if you keep my commandments and *endure to the end* you shall have eternal life, which gift is the greatest of all the gifts of God" (Doctrine and Covenants 14:6–7; emphasis added).

"He that is *faithful and endureth* shall overcome the world" (Doctrine and Covenants 63:47; emphasis added).

The word *valiant* derives from the Latin root *valere*—"be strong." Thus to endure valiantly denotes possessing or demon-strating consistent commitment, courage, and determination "in process of time" (Moses 7:21). We are to press forward and act as agents and not just sit passively as objects and wait to be acted upon. We are to endure valiantly, well, and with faith in the Lord

Jesus Christ. The power to become includes abiding, disciplined persistence in both the good and the bad of our mortal existence.

Elder Neal A. Maxwell explained: "Even yesterday's spiritual experience, however, does not guarantee us against tomorrow's relapse. Persistence thus matters greatly. More than a few, for instance, have had supernal, spiritual experiences only to fall away later; or, more often, merely to pull off to the side of the road, though only intending a brief rest stop.

"Hence, the emphasis on enduring well to the end is wise, simply because we are at risk till the end! By enduring well all along the way we can, for example, have felicity amid poverty and gratitude without plentitude. We can even have meekness amid injustice. One never sees the 'root of bitterness springing up' in enduring disciples (Hebrews 12:15)" (*If Thou Endure It Well*, 122).

A PATTERN IN ALL THINGS

In a revelation given through the Prophet Joseph Smith in June 1831, the Lord declared, "I will give unto you a pattern in all things, that ye may not be deceived; for Satan is abroad in the land, and he goeth forth deceiving the nations" (Doctrine and Covenants 52:14). Please consider one specific phrase in this verse: "a pattern in all things."

A pattern is a guide or a model. Patterns are used in sewing and knitting, in wood and metalworking, and in a wide variety of other productive pursuits, activities, and jobs. Patterns are used to prevent waste and unwanted deviations and facilitate uniformity that is appropriate and beneficial. Imagine the difficulty of sewing a blouse or building a piece of furniture without an appropriate pattern.

Vital spiritual patterns are evident in the life of the Savior, in the scriptures, and in the teachings of living prophets and apostles. These spiritual patterns are now and always have been important aids to discernment and sources of direction and protection for faithful Latter-day Saints. And spiritual patterns are essential in avoiding the deception that is so pervasive in our world today.

A powerful pattern the Lord uses to advance His work and to tutor Heavenly Father's children upon the earth is that of "small and simple things."

"Behold I say unto you, that by small and simple things are great things brought to pass; and small means in many instances doth confound the wise" (Alma 37:6).

"Wherefore, be not weary in well-doing, for ye are laying the foundation of a great work. And out of small things proceedeth that which is great" (Doctrine and Covenants 64:33).

This pattern is especially relevant for faithful disciples of the Savior who are striving to endure valiantly to the end.

Many people in our contemporary world are drawn to promises of big results that occur quickly and all at once. Consider, for example, all of the money spent on lottery tickets. Recall the claims of advertising messages you have received that pledge immediate weight loss, instant health, fast hair growth, and a more youthful appearance in just fourteen days. And we also are told that five quick and easy steps can help us grow spiritually in just three weeks. We are bombarded constantly with messages from a multiplicity of sources promoting instant gratification and outstanding performance that will impress our families and friends.

In a similar way, the adversary made impressive assertions about big results in premortality: "And I, the Lord God, spake unto Moses, saying: That Satan, whom thou hast commanded in the name of mine Only Begotten, is the same which was from the beginning, and he came before me, saying—Behold, here am I, send me, I will be thy son, and I will redeem all mankind, that one soul shall not be lost, and surely I will do it; wherefore give me thine honor" (Moses 4:1). Lucifer's grandiose pledge, however, was hollow and empty because he "sought to destroy the agency of man" (Moses 4:3).

In contrast to what we so often observe in the world, the Lord typically ministers "one by one" (3 Nephi 11:15). He enables us to learn "line upon line, precept upon precept, here a little and there a little" (2 Nephi 28:30). And He accomplishes His work by bringing to pass great things through small and simple means.

I believe many, if not all, of the most satisfying and memorable accomplishments in our homes, in the Church, in our jobs and professions, and in our communities will be the product of this important spiritual pattern—of simple and small things. We should find great comfort in the fact that ordinary people who faithfully, diligently, and consistently do simple things that are right before God will bring forth extraordinary results—as they appropriately seek for the power to become.

The following examples illustrate this truth.

Example 1: Conversion and Contribution

Luke Syphus and Christiana Long were born, respectively, in 1827 and 1832, and lived in England. Both Luke and Christiana received and studied the restored gospel of Jesus Christ and were baptized. Following their conversions, they met and courted, and they were married on Christmas Day, 1851. And approximately one year after their marriage, they boarded the ship *Java* and set sail for Australia.

During the five-month voyage, Luke and Christiana became good friends with Joseph and Adelaide Ridges. The Ridges couple likewise were immigrating to Australia from their native country of England. When the ship arrived at its destination in April 1853, the Syphus and Ridges families lived and worked together at Pennant Hills, approximately fifteen miles northwest of Sydney.

Luke and Christiana introduced Joseph and Adelaide to the restored gospel of Jesus Christ. During their journey from England, the Ridges family had grown to admire Luke and Christiana for their good habits, for their kindly ways, and for their example of strength and devotion as Brother and Sister Syphus faced the heartache associated with the death of their firstborn child. Luke loaned Joseph a copy of the Book of Mormon and a text of the teachings of Elder Orson Pratt. Both Joseph and Adelaide ultimately became convinced of the truthfulness of the gospel and were baptized in 1853 (see *Deseret News,* February 16, 1901).

As a child in England, Joseph Ridges had been fascinated by an organ factory near his home. He had spent long hours watching and learning how organs were constructed. In his spare time in Australia, using the skills he had developed in England, Joseph began to build a small, seven-stop pipe organ. The mission president, Augustus Farnham, suggested Brother Ridges donate the organ to the Church in Salt Lake City. Joseph agreed, and with the help of the members and missionaries he dismantled the organ, packed the parts into six large tin cases, and stowed the instrument in the cargo hold of a sailing vessel, the *Jenny Lind.* A company of approximately 120 people set sail for America in 1856, including the Ridges and Syphus families and the organ Joseph had constructed.

After landing in California, the organ was hauled across the desert by mule teams and arrived in Salt Lake City in June 1857. Brother Ridges installed the small organ in the old adobe tabernacle on Temple Square, where the Assembly Hall now stands. That simple instrument was the forerunner of a great organ Brother Ridges later was to build.

Construction began in the 1860s on the Tabernacle that stands today on Temple Square. Brigham Young asked Joseph, who at the time was farming in Provo, if he could build a large organ for the new building. Brother Ridges responded that he could, and the work began. Eventually the organ would have two manuals, 27 pedals, and 35 stops, with approximately 2,000 pipes—and it would measure 20 feet by 30 feet and stand 40 feet high. The organ took more than ten years to construct.

In this example we witness the power of a profound spiritual pattern—small and simple things bringing great things to pass. Acts of kindness, of righteous influence, and of Christian compassion by Luke and Christiana were instrumental in bringing to pass the conversions of Joseph and Adelaide. A small and simple organ in Australia helped to bring forth the great Tabernacle organ that today is one of the iconic symbols of The Church of Jesus Christ of Latter-day Saints. No big results occurred quickly or all at once. Rather, by small and simple things great things were brought to pass.

Example 2: Faith in the Savior

During my service as a stake president, I became acquainted with an adult man who received the message of the Restoration, was baptized and received the gift of the Holy Ghost, and was confirmed a member of the Church. He also received the Aaronic Priesthood and was ordained to the office of a priest. A retired military officer who had confronted many difficult events and circumstances in his life, he was a man of courage and bravery. Interestingly, however, this man of valor was scared to death to officiate as a priest at the sacrament table and offer a prayer on the emblems of the sacrament in front of a congregation. The fear he experienced was intense and almost paralyzing. But he prayed for help, he prepared, and he practiced. His simple faith in the Lord was evident in his action—in his prayers, in his preparation, and in his practice.

For several weeks this man would retire to a secluded area near his home, reverently kneel, and practice the blessings on the bread and on the water. He practiced over and over and over. He was blessed with the gift of faith that conquered his fear, and he eventually told the branch president he was ready to assume his responsibility at the sacrament table. The branch president called me following the sacrament meeting in which this man first blessed the sacrament. He indicated that words could not express the happiness and joy that were evident in the countenance of this good man as he sat with his family following the ordinance of the sacrament.

Faithful determination, heartfelt prayers, and patient persistence produced a seemingly ordinary but truly extraordinary spiritual result for this brother and his family. By small and simple things are great things brought to pass.

Example 3: Selfless Service

Our sons attended early-morning seminary at 6:00 a.m., and the classes were held in our ward building. The ward covered a very large geographic area, and many of the seminary students and their parents traveled long distances in the early-morning hours in order to attend.

One morning I dropped off our oldest son at the ward building for seminary. As he opened the door to get out of the car, I noticed a young mother sitting in the driver's seat of a van parked next to us. I also heard some unusual noises coming from the back of her van. I knew that this good sister lived approximately forty-five minutes away from the ward building, so I got out of my car to see if something was wrong with the van or if some assistance was needed.

As she rolled down her window to speak with me, I saw her other young children in the back of the van; some were eating snacks and others were playing or coloring. I most undiplomatically asked, "What in the world are you doing here this early with all of these kids?" She just smiled at me, and before she could respond to my question, I knew the answer. Her husband's job required him to be away from home Monday through Friday each week. Her oldest child was old enough to attend seminary but not old enough to drive a car. In the small community in which her family lived, there were no other members of the Church with whom she could carpool or coordinate rides. So early each morning she awakened all of her children, got them ready, and drove them to the ward building together so the oldest child could attend seminary. The mother and the other children waited in the van and played school until seminary was over. Only by following this pattern each morning could the oldest child attend seminary and have a ride back to school.

I have never forgotten what I felt and learned as I looked into the back of that van and answered for myself the question I had posed to this sister. That young mother was a most remarkable example of selfless service. She simply was willing to do whatever was necessary in order for her child to have the blessing of gospel instruction and the companionship of the Holy Ghost through seminary.

I have been blessed to observe many such people who in the process of time gradually have become more like the Savior through selfless service. There is a sanctifying and purifying power that can be received in no other way. By small and simple things shall great things be brought to pass.

Why Do Small and Simple Things Bring Great Things to Pass?

Please reflect on two important questions related to the principle of small and simple things:

1. Why do small and simple things bring great things to pass?

2. Why is the spiritual pattern of small and simple things bringing great things to pass so central to learning and living the gospel of Jesus Christ, to enduring to the end with faith and diligence, and to receiving the power to become?

We can learn much about the nature and importance of this spiritual pattern from the process of building or increasing physical stamina. One definition of *stamina* is having the energy and strength to maintain movement for a long period of time, whether persisting in an activity, event, illness, or challenging situation. When we refer to physical stamina, we commonly think of exercise, sports, workout regimens, or other physical activities. Increased physical stamina essentially means the human body can more easily withstand pain, fatigue, stress, and hardship. In simpler terms, stamina allows a person to exercise longer without resting.

People most commonly pursue the following steps to increase their physical stamina:

1. Lead an active life, including plenty of physical exercise for optimal health.
2. Drink plenty of water to keep the body hydrated.

3. Eat a healthy, balanced diet of a variety of vegetables, whole grains, lean meats, and fruits.

4. Visualize their goal.

5. Gradually and progressively build up to the target level of performance.

Building physical stamina takes time. The body must gradually get used to a more intense level of physical activity so that "burnout" does not occur in the early stages of the process. Increasing activity deliberately and steadily every day enables the body to improve its use of oxygen, increases lung capacity, and strengthens the muscle surrounding the heart, allowing it to pump more oxygen quicker.

Increasing physical stamina requires sustained focus and frequent effort, as opposed to occasional or intermittent bursts of intense activity. In like manner, if you and I are focused and consistent in developing our spiritual capacity, we can slowly and steadily strengthen our minds and hearts to discern, accept, and employ gospel truth; we can increase our spiritual capacity to detect and avoid temptation; and we can increase our determination and our ability to endure, through the enabling power of the Atonement, any challenges we encounter.

The spiritual pattern of small and simple things bringing forth great things produces firmness and steadfastness, deepening devotion, and more complete conversion to the Lord Jesus Christ and His gospel. As you and I become increasingly steadfast and immovable, we are less prone to zealous and exaggerated spurts of spirituality followed by extended periods of slackness. A spiritual "spurter" is one who is given to short bursts of spectacular effort followed by frequent and lengthy periods of rest.

A big spurt may appear to be impressive in the short run, but steadiness in small things over time is far more effective and far less dangerous, and it produces far more enduring results. Three consecutive days of fasting ultimately may not be as spiritually efficacious as three successive months of appropriate fasting and worship on the designated fast Sunday—of many small and simple things done consistently well. A great attempt to pray one time for five hours likely will not produce the spiritual results of meaningful morning and evening prayer offered consistently over five weeks—of many small and simple things done consistently well. And a single, great scripture-reading marathon cannot produce the spiritual impact of steady scripture study across many months.

President Spencer W. Kimball taught about the importance of small and simple things in our spiritual development and progress. In explicating the parable of the ten virgins he stated:

"The foolish [virgins] asked the others to share their oil, but spiritual preparedness cannot be shared in an instant. The wise had to go, else the bridegroom would have gone unwelcomed. They needed all their oil for themselves; they could not save the foolish. The responsibility was each for himself.

"This was not selfishness or unkindness. The kind of oil that is needed to illuminate the way and light up the darkness is not shareable. How can one share obedience to the principle of tithing; a mind at peace from righteous living; an accumulation of knowledge? How can one share faith or testimony? How can one share attitudes or chastity, or the experience of a mission? How can one share temple privileges? Each must obtain that kind of oil for himself.

"The foolish virgins were not averse to buying oil. They knew they should have oil. They merely procrastinated, not knowing when the bridegroom would come.

"In the parable, oil can be purchased at the market. In our

lives the oil of preparedness is accumulated drop by drop in righteous living. Attendance at sacrament meetings adds oil to our lamps, drop by drop over the years. Fasting, family prayer, home teaching, control of bodily appetites, preaching the gospel, studying the scriptures—each act of dedication and obedience is a drop added to our store. Deeds of kindness, payment of offerings and tithes, chaste thoughts and actions, marriage in the covenant for eternity—these, too, contribute importantly to the oil with which we can at midnight refuel our exhausted lamps" (*Faith Precedes the Miracle*, 255–56).

The key lesson for us to learn from the parable of the ten virgins is that deliberate and consistent preparation and performance provide essential oil for our lamps. By small and simple things are great things brought to pass.

Elder Neal A. Maxwell explained: "Measured steadiness is more efficient than spurts and then a slackening. Further, we are less apt to 'wear away' in prudent persistence than in a combination of breathlessness and ease. Sometimes we may reward our breathlessness with a respite that turns into a permanent repose; we do this by reflecting on all that we have done up to now and how it is surely now someone else's turn" (*Wherefore, Ye Must Press Forward*, 74).

In a gospel sense, we need to become focused and consistent in wisely building our spiritual stamina and avoid sporadic and shallow spiritual spurting. We can avoid or overcome unsustainable spiritual spurting as we employ the Lord's pattern of small and simple things and become valiant disciples with strong, spiritual stamina—blessed with capacity to endure to the end with faith in the Savior.

Enduring Valiantly—Key Principles

Two basic principles can bless and strengthen us as we strive to press forward and endure valiantly: (1) understanding our divine identity, and (2) discerning the intent of our enemy.

Understanding Our Divine Identity

Elder John A. Widtsoe stated: "The second greatest question of life was asked by the ancient Psalmist: 'What is man, that thou art mindful of him?' In importance, this query is next only to that concerning the nature of God. Inability to answer this question has often defeated fervent faith. The correct answer has enabled men and nations to build their futures securely. Faith has been most effective when accompanied by an understanding of man's relationship to Deity. The way out of the world's tragic chaos, the terror of poverty, sickness and war must be illuminated by a comprehension of man's nature and destiny" (in Conference Report, October 1936, 97).

"The Family: A Proclamation to the World" is a timely gift of knowledge about our divine identity from a loving Father to His children delivered through latter-day apostles and prophets. He has never left us to guess about what matters most in life, and He helps us to know who we are as His children and what we may become.

The First Presidency and the Quorum of the Twelve Apostles proclaimed:

"Marriage between a man and a woman is ordained of God and . . . the family is central to the Creator's plan for the eternal destiny of His children.

"All human beings—male and female—are created in the image of God. Each is a beloved spirit son or daughter of heavenly parents, and, as such, each has a divine nature and destiny. Gender is an essential characteristic of individual premortal, mortal, and eternal identity and purpose.

"In the premortal realm, spirit sons and daughters knew and worshipped God as their Eternal Father and accepted His plan by which His children could obtain a physical body and gain earthly experience to progress toward perfection and ultimately realize their divine destiny as heirs of eternal life. The divine plan of happiness enables family relationships to be perpetuated beyond the grave. Sacred ordinances and covenants available in holy temples make it possible for individuals to return to the presence of God and for families to be united eternally" ("The Family: A Proclamation to the World").

Importantly, the first three paragraphs of the proclamation provide answers to the greatest questions of life, as Elder Widtsoe defined those questions. Clearly, studying and pondering the doctrine contained in the proclamation will help each of us better understand the answer to the question, "What is man, that thou art mindful of him?" (Psalm 8:4) and provide an "anchor to [our] souls" (Ether 12:4) in the midst of troubling and perplexing times.

Knowing and understanding our divine identity as children of a loving Heavenly Father should influence everything about and relating to us—what we think, what we do, where we go, what we eat, what we drink, what we wear, and a multitude of other decisions and actions. Every aspect of our lives is influenced by a correct understanding of who we are and of our responsibility to be loyal to the royal within us. This fundamental truth is central to enduring valiantly to the end and becoming all that the Father and the Son yearn for us to become.

Understanding who and what we are as children of God has never been more important and more needed than it is today. Since the adversary always directs his most potent attacks at the doctrines, covenants, and ordinances that are of the greatest eternal worth, we should not be surprised to find one of Lucifer's prime targets is the truth about the nature and destiny of man.

President Boyd K. Packer has emphasized: "No greater ideal has been revealed than the supernal truth that we are the children of God, and we differ, by virtue of our creation, from all other living things. . . . No idea has been more *destructive* of happiness; no philosophy has produced more sorrow, more heartbreak and mischief; no idea has done more to destroy the family than the idea that we are not the offspring of God, only advanced animals, compelled to yield to every carnal urge" ("Our Moral Environment," 67; emphasis in original).

God is the supreme governor of the universe and the Father of mankind. When we speak of God, it is generally the Father to whom we refer, and all mankind are His children. Mankind has a special relationship to God that differentiates men and women from all other created things; we are literally God's offspring, made in His image, whereas all other things are the work of His hands (see Bible Dictionary, s.v. "God," 681–82).

The nature of this relationship between God and His children is highlighted in the Pearl of Great Price in the first chapter of the book of Moses. In this chapter God reveals Himself to and converses with Moses.

"The words of God, which he spake unto Moses at a time when Moses was caught up into an exceedingly high mountain,

"And he saw God face to face, and he talked with him, and the glory of God was upon Moses; therefore Moses could endure his presence" (Moses 1:1–2).

In verse three Moses begins to learn the answers to the greatest question of life—the question about the identity and nature of God. And in the first line of verse four, he begins to learn the answer to the second greatest question of life, the question of, "What is man?" (Psalm 8:4).

"And God spake unto Moses, saying: Behold, I am the Lord God Almighty, and Endless is my name; for I am without beginning of days or end of years; and is not this endless?

"And, behold, *thou art my son;* wherefore look, and I will show thee the workmanship of mine hands" (Moses 1:3–4; emphasis added).

The identity of Moses as a son of God is reiterated again powerfully in verses six and seven.

"And I have a work for thee, Moses, *my son;* and thou art in the similitude of mine Only Begotten; and mine Only Begotten is and shall be the Savior, for he is full of grace and truth. . . .

"And now, behold, this one thing I show unto thee, Moses, *my son* . . ." (Moses 1:6–7; emphasis added).

Three times God identifies Moses as His son.

The transfiguration concludes, the glory of God is no longer upon Moses, and he is left unto himself.

"And it came to pass that it was for the space of many hours before Moses did again receive his natural strength like unto man; and he said unto himself: Now, for this cause I know that man is nothing, which thing I never had supposed.

"But now mine own eyes have beheld God; but not my natural, but my spiritual eyes, for my natural eyes could not have beheld; for I should have withered and died in his presence; but his glory was upon me; and I beheld his face, for I was transfigured before him" (Moses 1:10–11).

"And it came to pass that when Moses had said these words, behold, Satan came tempting him, saying: Moses, son of man, worship me" (Moses 1:12). In essence, the adversary challenges Moses' understanding of his divine identity and potential: *You are not truly a son of God, Moses. You are just a man. There is nothing divine or distinctive in your heritage at all.*

"And it came to pass that Moses looked upon Satan and said: Who art thou? . . . *Behold, I am a son of God,* in the similitude of his Only Begotten; and where is thy glory, that I should worship thee?

"For behold, I could not look upon God, except his glory should come upon me, and I were transfigured before him. But I can look upon thee in the natural man. Is it not so, surely?" (Moses 1:13–14; emphasis added).

Significantly, Moses relies upon the knowledge of who he is as a son of Heavenly Father as a primary source of protection—and upon his experience with the glory of God to repudiate Satan's claims.

Moses then continues:

"Get thee hence, Satan; deceive me not; for God said unto me: Thou art after the similitude of mine Only Begotten. . . .

"And again Moses said: I will not cease to call upon God, I have other things to inquire of him: for his glory has been upon me, wherefore I can judge between him and thee. Depart hence, Satan" (Moses 1:16, 18).

Significantly, Satan challenges Moses a second time.

"And now, when Moses had said these words, Satan cried with a loud voice, and ranted upon the earth, and commanded, saying: I am the Only Begotten, worship me.

"And it came to pass that Moses began to fear exceedingly; and as he began to fear, he saw the bitterness of hell. Nevertheless, calling upon God, he received strength, and he commanded, saying: Depart from me, Satan, for this one God only will I worship, which is the God of glory" (Moses 1:19–20).

Satan then begins to tremble, and he departs.

This episode is most instructive. What was it that enabled Moses to withstand the fiery darts of the adversary? How was he able to resist the influence of the great deceiver? Moses knew his divine identity—that he was a child of God. Protective power flows from a correct understanding of who we are, of our relationship to God, and of our mortal purpose and eternal destiny.

The tactics of Lucifer are precisely the same today. The fundamental and frontal challenge remains the same: *You are not who you think you are. You are not what you have been taught. You are not really a son or daughter of God.* Moses was blessed and protected precisely because he learned, understood, and remembered who he was.

In our day, the assault on the fatherhood of God and the brotherhood and sisterhood of His children has grown more relentless, more bold, more direct, and more sophisticated. For example, we live at a time and in societies wherein the procreative powers bestowed upon us by a loving Father are viewed increasingly as a selfish and animalistic appetite to be satisfied "here and now" rather than as a sacred privilege and responsibility with eternal consequences. We live at a time wherein the family unit of a father and a mother and children, one of the central features of the Father's eternal plan of happiness, is viewed by many as antiquated and obsolete. And we live at a time wherein speaking the names of God the Eternal Father and of His Beloved Son Jesus Christ is ever more controversial in public settings. In spite of such influences and opposition, we can remain steadfast and strong as we remember always our divine identity and strive to be loyal to the royal within us.

The fourth chapter of Matthew in the New Testament contains another strong lesson about Satan's deceptive strategies and attacks on our divine identity. As the Savior prepared for His mortal ministry, He fasted for forty days and forty nights. (The corrections to the text contained in the Joseph Smith Translation of the Bible are inserted into the relevant verses in brackets.)

"And when he had fasted forty days and forty nights [and had communed with God], he was afterward an hungered, [and was left to be tempted of the devil,]

"And when the tempter came to him, he said, *If thou be the Son of God,* command that these stones be made bread.

"But he answered and said, It is written, Man shall not live by bread alone, but by every word that proceedeth out of the mouth of God.

"Then [Jesus was taken up into the holy city, and the Spirit setteth him on the pinnacle of the temple],

"[Then the devil came unto him and said,] *If thou be the Son of God,* cast thyself down: for it is written, He shall give his angels charge concerning thee: and in their hands they shall bear thee up, lest at any time thou dash thy foot against a stone. . . .

"[And again, Jesus was in the Spirit, and it taketh] him up into an exceeding high mountain, and sheweth him all the kingdoms of the world, and the glory of them;

"[And the devil came unto him again, and said,] All these things will I give thee, if thou wilt fall down and worship me.

"Then saith Jesus unto him, Get thee hence, Satan: for it is written, Thou shalt worship the Lord thy God, and him only shalt thou serve" (Matthew 4:2–10; emphasis added).

In our individual study and various classes at church we have learned that the bread described in these verses can represent the temptations of physical desires and appetites, that "casting thyself down" can symbolize the temptation of gaining worldly recognition and prominence, and that the kingdoms and glory of the world can stand for the temptations of wealth, power, position, and prestige.

Consider, however, that the three temptations to which we frequently refer in this episode are secondary in nature; they are not primary. The overarching and fundamental challenge to the Savior in each of these three confrontations is contained in the taunting statement, *"If thou be the Son of God."* Satan's strategy, in essence, was to dare the Son of God to inappropriately demonstrate His God-given powers and, thereby, forget who He was. The enticement from the adversary was to turn inward—feed thyself, seek recognition for thyself, and obtain worldly treasure for thyself. Because the character of Christ is to always turn outward in love and service to others, Satan was tempting the Lord to betray His divine identity, act contrary to His character, and turn inward. The adversary attempted to attack the Master's understanding of who He was and of His relationship with His Father. Thus, as the Savior prepared for and commenced His mortal ministry, the adversary assaulted His understanding of the answers to life's two greatest questions.

As His mortal ministry drew to a close, Jesus was accused and condemned before Pilate, mocked, and crucified. Please remember that the Savior of the world was about to complete the atoning sacrifice. The Lord had been betrayed and physically battered; He had "trodden the wine-press alone" (Doctrine and Covenants 76:107). Given His agony in the Garden of Gethsemane and His torture on the cross, there had been, perhaps, no time in His earthly ministry when He was more physically exhausted, spiritually spent, and emotionally drained. Obviously, the adversary knew that he had only one last chance to thwart the plan of the Father and interrupt the Atonement. Given the Savior's condition and Satan's ultimate desperation, what temptation and strategy would the arch deceiver employ?

"Then were there two thieves crucified with him, one on the right hand, and another on the left.

"And they that passed by reviled him, wagging their heads,

"And saying, Thou that destroyest the temple, and buildest it in three days, save thyself. *If thou be the Son of God,* come down from the cross.

"Likewise also the chief priests mocking him, with the scribes and elders, said,

"He saved others; himself he cannot save. *If he be the King of Israel,* let him now come down from the cross, and we will believe him.

"He trusted in God; let him deliver him now, *if he will have him:* for he said, I am the Son of God.

"The thieves also, which were crucified with him, cast the same in his teeth" (Matthew 27:38–44; emphasis added).

The last and most potent of the fiery darts Lucifer could direct at the Savior, just as he had attempted at the beginning of the Master's mortal ministry, was aimed at the answers to life's two greatest questions. With all of his diabolical designs hanging in the balance, Satan again hurled the sneering challenges of "If thou be the Son of God," "If he be the King of Israel," and "if he will have him." Interestingly, in this final scene the tempting taunts came through other people and not directly from the adversary.

Satan inevitably will use this identical strategy and similar tactics on each of us, especially as we strive to endure valiantly in troubled and troubling times. He would have us conclude that God is not our Eternal Father, and therefore He cannot possibly be mindful of us. However, the scriptures and living apostles and prophets teach and testify that indeed we are children of God, that "he has sent [us] here, has given [us] an earthly home with parents kind and dear" ("I Am a Child of God," *Hymns,* no. 301). Just as the Savior was strengthened through a correct understanding of who He was and His relationship with the Eternal Father, so we likewise can be blessed and protected by and through these eternal truths.

"What is man, that thou are mindful of him?" (Psalm 8:4). We are sons and daughters of God. "Rich blessings are in store; if [we] but learn to do his will, [we'll] live with him once more" ("I Am a Child of God," *Hymns,* no. 301).

Discerning the Intent of the Adversary

The lessons that can be learned from repeated study of the war chapters in the Book of Mormon have great value and applicability for us in the latter days as we strive to endure valiantly to the end. A number of episodes in this sacred volume of scripture highlight the truth that accurate awareness of an enemy's intent leads to appropriate preparations for battle.

In the book of Alma, for example, we read how Amlici incited his followers to rebel against the established pattern of governing "by the voice of the people" (Alma 2:3) and install him as the king.

"And it came to pass that the people assembled themselves together throughout all the land, every man according to his mind, whether it were for or against Amlici, in separate bodies, having much dispute and wonderful contentions one with another.

"And thus they did assemble themselves together to cast in their voices concerning the matter; and they were laid before the judges.

"And it came to pass that the voice of the people came against Amlici, that he was not made king over the people" (Alma 2:5–7).

But the voice of the people did not diminish Amlici's ambitions.

"Amlici did stir up those who were in his favor to anger against those who were not in his favor.

"And it came to pass that they gathered themselves together, and did consecrate Amlici to be their king.

"Now when Amlici was made king over them he commanded them that they should take up arms against their brethren; and this he did that he might subject them to him" (Alma 2:8–10).

Note the lesson contained in verses twelve and thirteen: "Therefore the people of the Nephites were *aware of the intent* of the Amlicites, and *therefore they did prepare to meet them;* yea, *they did arm themselves* with swords, and with cimeters, and with bows, and with arrows, and with stones, and with slings, and with all manner of weapons of war, of every kind.

"*And thus they were prepared* to meet the Amlicites *at the time of their coming*" (Alma 2:12–13; emphasis added).

In our day we do not fight with swords, cimeters, bows, arrows, and stones. Rather, we rely upon the protecting power of sacred ordinances and covenants, "the virtue of the word of God" (Alma 31:5) and "feasting upon the word of Christ" (2 Nephi 31:20; 32:3), individual and family prayer, family home evening, and consecrated service.

Devoted disciples also take upon themselves "the whole armour of God, that ye may be able to withstand in the evil day, and having done all, to stand.

"Stand therefore, having your loins girt about with truth, and having on the breastplate of righteousness;

"And your feet shod with the preparation of the gospel of peace;

"Above all, taking the shield of faith, wherewith ye shall be able to quench all the fiery darts of the wicked.

"And take the helmet of salvation, and the sword of the Spirit, which is the word of God" (Ephesians 6:13–17).

Thus, understanding the intent of an enemy is a key prerequisite to effective preparation and enables us to effectively "meet [our opponents] at the time of their coming." We do not fear surprise attacks or being caught off guard. As we learn from the Nephites, awareness, preparation, and timeliness provide both protection and peace.

In another episode, Alma and Amulek proclaimed the gospel in Ammonihah and called the people to repentance.

"But behold, I say unto you that if ye persist in your wickedness that your days shall not be prolonged in the land, for the Lamanites shall be sent upon you; and if ye repent not *they shall come in a time when you know not,* and ye shall be visited with utter destruction; and it shall be according to the fierce anger of the Lord" (Alma 9:18; emphasis added).

Alma warned that wickedness would constrain both the awareness and the preparation of the Nephites. Thus, righteousness is essential if we are to qualify for and receive the protecting blessings of the Lord.

Alma and his sons also went forth to preach the gospel at the time the Zoramites and other Nephite dissenters became Lamanites. Moroni, the military leader of the Nephites, made preparations to battle against the growing Lamanite armies and equipped his warriors with innovative defensive armor (see Alma 43:16–23). All of Moroni's plans and tactics grew out of his understanding of the intent of the enemy.

"And now, as *Moroni knew the intention of the Lamanites,* that it was their intention to destroy their brethren, or to subject them and bring them into bondage that they might establish a kingdom unto themselves over all the land;

"And he also knowing that it was the only desire of the Nephites to preserve their lands, and their liberty, and their church, therefore he thought it no sin that he should defend them by stratagem; therefore, he found by his spies which course the Lamanites were to take.

"Therefore, he divided his army and brought a part over into the valley, and concealed them on the east, and on the south of the hill Riplah;

"And the remainder he concealed in the west valley, on the west of the river Sidon, and so down into the borders of the land Manti.

"And thus having placed his army according to his desire, *he was prepared to meet them*" (Alma 43:29–33; emphasis added).

Please note that Moroni formulated both defensive and offensive strategies based upon his knowledge about the intent of the enemy, and his design was established upon a righteous cause.

An additional example from the book of Alma emphasizes the importance of diligent and inspired preparation of our "places of security." The invading Lamanites were unable to take the fortified cities of Ammonihah and Noah because of the preparatory measures directed by Captain Moroni.

"Behold, I said that the city of Ammonihah had been rebuilt. I say unto you, yea, that it was in part rebuilt; and because the Lamanites had destroyed it once because of the iniquity of the people, they supposed that it would again become an easy prey for them.

"But behold, how great was their disappointment; for behold, the Nephites had dug up a ridge of earth round about them, which was so high that the Lamanites could not cast their stones and their arrows at them that they might take effect, neither could they come upon them save it was by their place of entrance.

"Now at this time the chief captains of the Lamanites were astonished exceedingly, because of *the wisdom of the Nephites in preparing their places of security*" (Alma 49:3–5; emphasis added).

Examples of "places of security" for us today can be our families and homes, our righteous patterns and practices, and our stakes, districts, wards, and branches.

"Now the leaders of the Lamanites had supposed, because of the greatness of their numbers, yea, they supposed that they should be privileged to come upon them as they had hitherto done; yea, and they had also prepared themselves with shields, and with breastplates; and they had also prepared themselves with garments of skins, yea, very thick garments to cover their nakedness.

"And being thus prepared they supposed that they should easily overpower and subject their brethren to the yoke of bondage, or slay and massacre them according to their pleasure.

"But behold, to their uttermost astonishment, they were prepared for them, *in a manner which never had been known* among the children of Lehi. Now they were prepared for the Lamanites, to battle after the manner of the instructions of Moroni.

"And it came to pass that the Lamanites, or the Amalickiahites, were *exceedingly astonished at their manner of preparation for war*" (Alma 49:6–9; emphasis added).

The diligence and faithfulness of the Nephites produced a manner of preparation that was inspired, innovative, and effective. And such results are available to us in the latter days as we press forward along the pathway of perfection in the journey of mortality.

The intent of our enemy in the latter-day war in which we are engaged is quite clear. The Father's plan is designed to provide direction for His children, to help them become happy, and to bring them safely home to Him with resurrected, exalted bodies. Heavenly Father desires us to be together in the light and filled with hope. In contrast, Lucifer labors to make the sons and daughters of God confused and unhappy and to hinder their eternal progression. The overarching intent of the father of lies is that all of us might become "miserable like unto himself" (2 Nephi 2:27). Lucifer wants us ultimately to be alone in the dark and without hope.

Satan relentlessly works to distort the most important elements of the Father's plan. He does not have a body, and his eternal progress has been halted. Just as water flowing in a riverbed is stopped by a dam, so the adversary's eternal progress is thwarted because he does not have a physical body. Because of his rebellion, Lucifer has denied himself all of the mortal blessings and experiences made possible through a body of flesh and bones. He cannot learn the lessons that only an embodied spirit can learn. He resents the reality of a literal and universal Resurrection of all mankind. One of the potent scriptural meanings of the word *damned* is illustrated in his inability to continue developing and becoming like our Heavenly Father.

Because a physical body is so central to the Father's plan of happiness and our spiritual development, Lucifer seeks to frustrate our progression by tempting us to use our bodies improperly. One of the ultimate ironies of eternity is that the adversary, who is miserable precisely because he has no physical body, entices us to share in his misery through the improper use of our bodies. The very tool he does not have is thus the primary target of his attempts to lure us to spiritual destruction.

The adversary also attacks other central elements of the Father's plan—specifically, the importance of marriage and family. His battle plan was established long ago, his forces are numerous and well equipped, and he commands and fights fiercely. However, he will not win the war! Our victory is assured as we faithfully honor

covenants and rely upon the merits, mercy, and grace of the Holy
Messiah.

"In the strength of the Lord did we go forth to battle against
the [enemy]; for [we] did cry mightily to the Lord that he would
deliver us out of the hands of our enemies, for we were awakened
to a remembrance of the deliverance of our fathers" (Mosiah 9:17).

"I tell you these things because of your prayers; wherefore, treasure up wisdom in your bosoms, lest the wickedness of men reveal
these things unto you by their wickedness, in a manner which shall
speak in your ears with a voice louder than that which shall shake
the earth; but *if ye are prepared ye shall not fear*" (Doctrine and
Covenants 38:30; emphasis added).

Summary

The Lord declared in the early days of this dispensation, "I will
give unto you a pattern in all things, that ye may not be deceived;
for Satan is abroad in the land, and he goeth forth deceiving the
nations" (Doctrine and Covenants 52:14). In a world of increasing
wickedness, in a world where good is called evil and evil is called
good, in a world that confuses "darkness for light, and light for darkness" (2 Nephi 15:20), we can be blessed with "the hope of righteousness" (Galatians 5:5), "the light of the Lord" (Isaiah 2:5), and
protection against deception (see 1 Nephi 15:24; Helaman 5:12).

As the Savior declared, "Wherefore, be not weary in well-
doing, for ye are laying the foundation of a great work. And out
of *small things* proceedeth that which is great" (Doctrine and
Covenants 64:33; emphasis added).

As we learn and understand who we are as sons and daughters
of God, and as we are blessed with discernment about the intent

of our enemies, we can be blessed to endure valiantly and well. Challenges and trials will not be eliminated from our lives, but through the Atonement of Jesus Christ our spiritual strength and capacity will be increased and enlarged.

The imagery suggested in the Doctrine and Covenants is most instructive: "You know, brethren, that a very large ship is benefited very much by a *very small helm* in the time of a storm, by being kept workways with the wind and the waves.

"Therefore, dearly beloved brethren, let us *cheerfully* do all things that lie in our power; and then may we stand still, with the utmost assurance, to see the salvation of God, and for his arm to be revealed" (Doctrine and Covenants 123:16–17; emphasis added).

Truly, we can press forward along the pathway to perfection with steadfastness in the Savior, a perfect brightness of hope, and a love of God and of all mankind. And as we feast upon the words of Christ and endure valiantly to the end, the promise is that we shall have eternal life (see 2 Nephi 31:20).

> *Press forward, Saints, with steadfast faith in Christ,*
> *With hope's bright flame alight in heart and mind,*
> *With love of God and love of all mankind.*
> *Alleluia!*
>
> *Press forward, feasting on the word of Christ.*
> *Receive his name, rejoicing in his might.*
> *Come unto God; find everlasting light.*
> *Alleluia!*
>
> *Press on, enduring in the ways of Christ.*
> *His love proclaim thru days of mortal strife.*
> *Thus saith our God: "Ye have eternal life!"*
> *Alleluia!*
> ("Press Forward, Saints," Hymns, *no. 81)*

Related Readings

1. Henry B. Eyring, "The Power of Deliverance," BYU Devotional, January 15, 2008. Available online at speeches.byu.edu.

2. Dallin H. Oaks, "The Dedication of a Lifetime," CES Devotional, May 1, 2005. Available online at lds.org.

3. Jeffrey R. Holland, "Cast Not Away Therefore Your Confidence," BYU Devotional, March 2, 1999. Available online at speeches.byu.edu.

4. Dallin H. Oaks, "Our Strengths Can Become Our Downfall," BYU Fireside, June 7, 1992. Available online at speeches.byu.edu.

5. Harold B. Lee, "Be Loyal to the Royal within You," BYU Devotional, September 11, 1973. Available online at speeches.byu.edu.

6. Marvin J. Ashton, "In His Strength," *Ensign,* July 1973, 24–27.

7. Gordon B. Hinckley, "The Loneliness of Leadership," BYU Devotional, November 4, 1969. Available online at speeches.byu.edu.

8. J. Reuben Clark Jr., "To Them of the Last Wagon," in Conference Report, October 1947, 154–60.

Explore these concepts further with a group discussion.

Scan this code or visit seek.deseretbook.com/powertobecome

CONSIDER

In what ways can the Lord's pattern of "small and simple things" enhance my capacity to "endure valiantly"?

CONSIDER

What am I learning about the role and power of my divine identity in my life?

CONSIDER

How can discerning the "intent of the enemy" help me to better prepare and fortify my "places of security"?

My Own Questions to Consider

SCRIPTURES RELATED TO WHAT I AM LEARNING

AN INVITATION TO LEARN, TO ACT, AND TO BECOME		
What additional doctrines and principles, if understood, would help me to endure valiantly?	What can and should I do to act in those doctrines and principles?	How will I know if I am making progress in striving to become more like the Savior?

AN INVITATION TO LEARN, TO ACT, AND TO BECOME		
What additional doctrines and principles, if understood, would help me to endure valiantly?	What can and should I do to act in those doctrines and principles?	How will I know if I am making progress in striving to become more like the Savior?

An Invitation to Learn, to Act, and to Become		
What additional doctrines and principles, if understood, would help me to endure valiantly?	What can and should I do to act in those doctrines and principles?	How will I know if I am making progress in striving to become more like the Savior?

CHAPTER 5

POWER TO BECOME AND ALL THINGS GATHERED TOGETHER IN ONE

As disciples of the Lord Jesus Christ, our individual responsibility is to learn what we should learn, to act and live as we know we should act and live, and to become what the Master would have us become. These three fundamental and interrelated gospel imperatives—learning, acting, and becoming—are central to our spiritual development and happiness in mortality and our progress throughout eternity.

Precious perspective and expanded spiritual capacity result from "gather[ing] together in one all things in Christ, both which are in heaven, and which are on earth; even in him" (Ephesians 1:10). The power of the Savior's gospel to bless and guide us comes from the connectedness and interrelatedness of its doctrines, principles, and practices. Only as we *gather together in one* all things in Christ can we diligently strive to become what God desires us to become (see Matthew 5:48; 3 Nephi 12:48) and endure valiantly to the end.

While the Lord seeks to gather all things together in one, we may often segment, specialize, and apply gospel truths in our lives in ways that limit our understanding and vision. Such an approach constrains the purification, the joy, the continuing conversion, and the spiritual power and protection that come from "yielding [our] hearts unto God" (Helaman 3:35). Simply performing and dutifully checking off all of the things on our lengthy gospel "to do" list do not necessarily enable us to receive His image in our countenances or bring about the mighty change of heart (see Alma 5:14).

In this concluding chapter, I attempt to "gather all things together in one" by reviewing briefly the sequence and basic concepts and principles presented in each of the chapters in *Increase in Learning, Act in Doctrine,* and *Power to Become.* The repetition of key truths is intentional, as repetition is an important principle of effective gospel learning.

Increase in Learning: Spiritual Patterns for Obtaining Your Own Answers

You and I are here upon the earth to prepare for eternity, to learn how to learn, to learn things that are temporally important and eternally essential, and to assist others in learning wisdom and truth (see Doctrine and Covenants 97:1). Understanding who we are, where we came from, and why we are upon the earth places upon each of us a great responsibility both to learn how to learn and to learn to love learning.

An Individual Responsibility to Learn

Each and every member of The Church of Jesus Christ of Latter-day Saints bears a *personal* responsibility to learn and live the truths of the Savior's restored gospel and to receive by proper authority the ordinances of salvation. We should not expect the Church as an organization to teach or tell us all of the things we need to know and do to become devoted disciples and endure valiantly to the end (see Doctrine and Covenants 121:29). The moral agency afforded to all of Father's children through the plan of salvation and the Atonement of Jesus Christ is divinely designed to facilitate our individual and independent learning, acting, and, ultimately, becoming.

Spiritual knowledge cannot be given by or borrowed from another person. Shortcuts to the desired destination do not exist. Cramming for the ultimate final examination on the day of judgment is not an option. In this eternally important endeavor, the Lord's pattern is "line upon line, precept upon precept, here a little and there a little; and blessed are those who hearken unto my precepts, and lend an ear unto my counsel, for they shall *learn* wisdom; for unto him that receiveth I will give more" (2 Nephi 28:30; emphasis added). The efficacy of the law of the harvest clearly applies to our individual responsibility to learn and live gospel truths: "For whatsoever a man soweth, that shall he also reap" (Galatians 6:7).

Knowledge, Understanding, and Intelligence

A hierarchy of importance exists among the things you and I can learn. Indeed, all information and knowledge are not equally important. The Apostle Paul taught this truth in his second epistle to Timothy as he warned that in the latter days many people would be "ever learning, and never able to come to the knowledge of the truth" (2 Timothy 3:7).

Many facts are helpful or merely interesting to know. Some knowledge is useful to learn and apply. But gospel truths are essential for us to understand and live if we are to become what our Heavenly Father yearns for us to become.

Knowledge refers generally to facts, information, and abilities obtained through experience or education. Using the instrument of our physical bodies and our capacity to reflect and reason, we can gather and analyze facts, organize and interpret information, gain and learn from experience, and identify patterns and relationships. Of the many types of knowledge that can be acquired, spiritual knowledge is the most important—both in mortality and in eternity.

Understanding is the keystone that is erected upon the cornerstone of knowledge and precedes intelligence. Interestingly, the word *understanding* is commonly described in the scriptures in relation to the heart. *Understanding* as used in the scriptures does not refer solely or even primarily to intellectual or cognitive comprehension. Rather, when the Holy Ghost confirms in our hearts as true what we know in our minds, understanding occurs.

We begin to obtain understanding and experience a mighty change of heart as testimony and conviction move from our heads to our hearts. Thoughts and feelings put into our hearts by the Holy Ghost (see Doctrine and Covenants 100:5–8; 8:2) are a result of the spiritual gift of revelation. Understanding, then, is a revealed conclusion and a spiritual gift.

Intelligence is the righteous application of knowledge and understanding in action and judgment. It is the capstone that is constructed upon the cornerstone of knowledge and made stable by the keystone of understanding. Righteous action grows out of understanding. You and I may know the right things to do, but intelligence involves more than just knowing. If you and I are intelligent, we will consistently do the right things. Intelligence is living in such a way that the doctrines of the gospel are an active and integral part of who we are, and what we are, and what we do, and what we think.

In section 1 of the Doctrine and Covenants, the Savior describes this Church as "the only true and living church upon the face of the . . . earth" (Doctrine and Covenants 1:30). What is it that truly makes The Church of Jesus Christ of Latter-day Saints a living Church? It is a living Savior, the gift of the Holy Ghost and the attendant spiritual blessings and gifts, and the authority and power of the priesthood that make His Church both true and living. Appropriately seeking for knowledge, understanding, and intelligence is essential for each of us to become a living member of the Savior's living Church.

"For intelligence cleaveth unto intelligence; wisdom receiveth wisdom; truth embraceth truth; virtue loveth virtue; light cleaveth unto light" (Doctrine and Covenants 88:40).

Prayerful Inquiry: Asking, Seeking, and Knocking

Inquire is an action word that denotes asking, requesting, petitioning, soliciting, investigating, and exploring. Inquiring of the Lord requires from us much more than merely or routinely asking; it is a spiritually demanding and rigorous process. Sincere desire, diligent preparation, earnest repentance, and faithful confidence in and commitment to act upon the expected instruction precede prayerful inquiry. Thus, inquiring of the Lord includes asking, but asking alone is not all that is involved in inquiring. Prayerful inquiry is a necessary prerequisite to inspiration and revelation.

Three components of prayerful inquiry are emphasized repeatedly in the scriptures: asking, seeking, and knocking. These three active components of prayerful inquiry denote initiating, engaging anxiously, pressing forward steadfastly, and acting. Asking, seeking, and knocking are interrelated, overlapping, and vital elements in the pattern the Lord has employed when giving direction, instruction, and revelation. Honesty, effort, commitment, and persistence are required in asking, seeking, and knocking.

The principle of prayerful inquiry and the pattern of asking, seeking, and knocking enable us to obtain the knowledge, understanding, and intelligence that are essential to becoming living members of the Lord's living Church and suggest three basic responsibilities for each of us as latter-day learners. First, inquiring of the Lord through asking, seeking, and knocking requires and is an expression of faith in the Savior. Second, we should be simultaneously persisting in and remaining patient with this active process. Third, discerning and accepting the will of God in our lives are fundamental elements of prayerful inquiry through asking, seeking, and knocking.

"But continue thou in the things which thou hast learned and hast been assured of, knowing of whom thou hast learned them" (2 Timothy 3:14).

"Learn of me, and listen to my words; walk in the meekness of my Spirit, and you shall have peace in me" (Doctrine and Covenants 19:23).

Doctrines, Principles, and Applications: A Framework for Gospel Learning

Learning is central to the plan of salvation, to our happiness in mortality, and to our eternal progress. A basic and flexible framework for learning about gospel learning includes three basic elements: doctrines, principles, and applications.

A gospel doctrine is a truth—a truth of salvation revealed by a loving Heavenly Father. Gospel doctrines are eternal, do not change, and pertain to the eternal progression and exaltation of Heavenly Father's sons and daughters. Doctrines such as the nature of the Godhead, the plan of happiness, and the Atonement of Jesus Christ are foundational, fundamental, and comprehensive.

Gospel doctrines answer the question of "why?" For example, the doctrine of the plan of happiness answers the question of *why* we are here upon the earth. The doctrine of the Atonement explains *why* Jesus is our mediator and advocate with the Father. Basic gospel doctrines are the spiritual foundation for all that we learn, teach, and do—and a vital source of power and strength as we strive to become what the Lord would have us become.

A gospel principle is a doctrinally based guideline for the righteous exercise of moral agency. Principles are subsets or components of broader gospel truths and provide direction. Correct principles always are based upon and arise from doctrines, do not change, and answer the question of "what?" Many principles can grow out of and be associated with a single doctrine. For example, the doctrine of the plan of happiness gives rise to such principles as obedience, service, and progression.

A principle is not a behavior or a specific action. Rather, principles provide basic guidelines for behavior and action.

Applications are the actual behaviors, action steps, practices, or procedures by which gospel doctrines and principles are enacted in our lives. Whereas doctrines and principles do not change, applications appropriately can vary according to needs and circumstances. Applications answer the question of "how?" Many applications can grow out of and be associated with a single principle.

The framework of doctrines, principles, and applications is a flexible tool that can be used to enhance our gospel learning. It is not a rigid set of definitions or a formula that leads to "correct" answers about which applications and principles are associated with particular gospel doctrines. Rather, it can be a useful aid as we apply the principle of prayerful inquiry and the pattern of asking, seeking, and knocking. If we focus on asking the right questions, we are much more likely to obtain inspired and insightful answers as we work, ponder, search, and pray.

Our tendency as members of the Church is to focus on applications. But as we learn to ask ourselves, "What doctrines and principles, if understood, would help with this challenge?" we come to realize that the answers always are in the doctrines and principles of the gospel.

ACT IN DOCTRINE: SPIRITUAL PATTERNS FOR TURNING FROM SELF TO THE SAVIOR

As we seek for the companionship of the Holy Ghost and strive faithfully to fulfill our personal responsibility to "increase in learning" (Proverbs 9:9), we more consistently "act in doctrine" (Doctrine and Covenants 101:78).

The word *act* denotes performing, behaving, and living. The doctrine of Christ is revealed truth that pertains to our eternal progression and happiness. Thus, to "act in doctrine" is to live according to and "in" revealed truth.

The process of effectively doing and living what we know to be true is one of the great challenges of mortality. Unfortunately for all of us, what we learn and know is not always reflected in what we do. As disciples of the Savior, we are not merely striving to know more; rather, we need to consistently do more of what we know is right and become better. "If ye know these things, happy are ye if ye do them" (John 13:17).

The Character of Christ

As described in *Lectures on Faith,* one of the three things "necessary in order that any rational and intelligent being may exercise faith in [the Father and Son] unto life and salvation" is "a correct idea of [Their] character, perfections, and attributes" (page 38). Thus, the name, the character, and the Atonement of the Lord Jesus Christ lead us to the Father and are the basis for and ultimate source of a mighty change of heart (see Alma 5:12–14), of strong testimony, of deepening conversion, and of dedicated discipleship. To "increase in learning" (Proverbs 9:9–10) about the Savior's character is the essential first step if we are to reduce the gap between what we know and what we do, faithfully and more consistently "act in doctrine" (Doctrine and Covenants 101:78), receive the "power of his word . . . in us" (Alma 26:13), and truly "come unto Christ" (Moroni 10:32).

One of the greatest indicators of righteous character is the capacity to recognize and appropriately respond to other people who are experiencing the very challenge or adversity that is most immediately and forcefully pressing upon us. Character is revealed, for example, in the power to discern the suffering of other people when we ourselves are suffering; in the ability to detect the hunger of others when we are hungry; and in the power to reach out and extend compassion for the spiritual agony of others when we are in the midst of our own spiritual distress. Therefore, character is demonstrated by looking, turning, and reaching outward when the instinctive response of the "natural man" (Mosiah 3:19) in each of us is to turn inward and to be selfish and self-absorbed. And the Savior of the world is the source, the standard, and the ultimate criterion of moral character and the perfect example of charity and consistency. The Lord's divine character is revealed repeatedly in the holy scriptures.

We can in mortality seek to be blessed with and develop essential elements of a Christlike character. Indeed, it is possible for us as mortals to strive in righteousness to receive the spiritual gifts associated with the capacity to reach outward even in our own times of distress. We cannot obtain such a capacity through sheer willpower or personal determination. Rather, we need and are dependent upon "the merits, and mercy, and grace of the Holy Messiah" (2 Nephi 2:8). But "line upon line, precept upon precept" (2 Nephi 28:30) and in the process of time (see Moses 7:21), we can increasingly reach outward when the natural tendency is for us to turn inward.

As we strive to have "this mind be in [us], which was also in Christ Jesus" (Philippians 2:5), we readily recognize that what we know about the Savior and His restored gospel is not always reflected in what we do and how we live. And the essential first step in reducing the disparity between gospel knowledge and righteous behavior is learning about and emulating the character of Christ.

Moral Agency

The gift of moral agency is central in the Father's plan of happiness and a supernal blessing. Agency enables the sons and daughters of God to be "agents unto themselves" (Doctrine and Covenants 58:28) and is the source of our capacity to "act in doctrine."

In the premortal council, Lucifer "sought to destroy the agency of man" (Moses 4:3). If agency were nullified, then no sins or transgressions ever would have been committed by the sons and daughters of God—thus, no fall of Adam and no individual sins. Without agency, learning and growing and developing would not be possible. If no sins or transgressions were committed, then the law of justice would not be violated. And if the law of justice were not violated, then there would be no need for a redeeming sacrifice to meet the demands of the law.

Lucifer aspired to the glory of the Father (see Moses 4:1). He had absolutely no concern for or interest in our welfare; he only wanted to use us to selfishly get something for himself. Satan is impatient, impulsive, impetuous, and intolerant—and "he seeketh that all men might be miserable like unto himself" (2 Nephi 2:27).

A covenant is an agreement between God and His children upon the earth, and it is important to recognize that God determines the conditions of all gospel covenants. You and I do not select or choose the elements of a covenant. Rather, exercising our moral agency, we accept the terms and requirements of a covenant as our Eternal Father has established them (see Bible Dictionary, s.v. "Covenant," 651).

The act of exercising agency and entering into a covenant with God—for example, the covenant associated with the ordinance of baptism—commences a gradual and eternally important transformation. As we turn to the Savior and away from selfishness and sin, we start to "[put] off the natural man" (Mosiah 3:19). We begin the process of becoming a saint (see Mosiah 3:19) by humbly emulating and striving to obtain the character of Christ as we turn to obedience and righteousness, deny ourselves, take up His cross, and follow Him (see Matthew 16:24; Mark 8:34; Luke 9:23).

As we turn to the Savior and away from self through covenants, we in essence bind ourselves to act in doctrine.

Many times the disparity between what we know about the doctrines and principles of the Savior's restored gospel and how we live is caused by incomplete or inaccurate knowledge. A correct understanding of the Father's plan of happiness, of the Atonement, of moral agency, and of covenants is essential for every member of The Church of Jesus Christ of Latter-day Saints. As we increase in learning about these basic truths, our capacity to act in doctrine is enlarged, extended, and strengthened.

A familiar hymn is entitled "Choose the Right" for a reason. We have not been blessed with agency to choose whatever we want whenever we will. Rather, moral agency enables us as agents to turn from self to the Savior, to pledge our willingness to take His name upon us, to love one another and choose God, and to bind ourselves to faithfully act in His doctrine.

Conversion to the Lord

As we increase in learning, turn to the Savior, and act in doctrine, our personal testimonies of Him and of His gospel are strengthened and we become more fully converted.

A testimony is personal knowledge of spiritual truth. A testimony is the result of the Holy Ghost confirming the reality of truth to our souls (see Moroni 10:4–5). Fundamental components of a testimony include the knowledge that Heavenly Father lives and loves us, that Jesus Christ is our Redeemer and Savior, and that the gospel of Jesus Christ is true and has been restored to the earth in its fulness in the latter days.

The knowledge and spiritual conviction we receive from the Holy Ghost are the result of revelation. Seeking for and obtaining these blessings require a sincere heart, real intent, and faith in the Lord Jesus Christ (see Moroni 10:4). And such a personal testimony also brings responsibility, duty, and accountability.

Conversion is described in the scriptures as putting off the natural man (see Mosiah 3:19), experiencing a mighty change of heart (see Alma 5:12–14), undergoing a spiritual rebirth (see Mosiah 27:24–25), and becoming a new creature in Christ (see 2 Corinthians 5:17). Please note that the conversion described in these verses is mighty, not minor—a spiritual rebirth and fundamental change of what we think and feel, what we desire and do, and what we are and strive to become. Indeed, the essence of the gospel of Jesus Christ entails a fundamental and permanent change in our very nature made possible through the Atonement of the Savior. As we turn to and follow the Master, we choose to change our hearts—to be spiritually reborn.

Knowing by the power of the Holy Ghost that Jesus is the Christ is a good, an important, and a necessary thing. But earnestly coming unto Him and giving our whole souls as an offering requires much more than merely knowing. Continuing conversion requires all of our heart, all of our mind, and all of our might and strength (see Doctrine and Covenants 4:2).

A testimony is the beginning of and a prerequisite to conversion unto the Lord. A testimony is a point of departure; it is not an ultimate destination. A strong testimony is the necessary foundation upon which conversion is established. A testimony is the initial step on the pathway of ongoing and deepening conversion.

Whereas a testimony is spiritual knowledge of truth obtained through the power of the Holy Ghost, conversion is deepening devotion to and consistent application of the knowledge we have received. Knowing that the gospel is true is the essence of testimony. Consistently being true to the gospel we know is the essence of conversion. We can be constant and true to many worthwhile things, but ultimately we must be converted unto the Lord and the things that are spiritually and eternally essential. We should both know the gospel is true and constantly be true to the gospel.

As we come to a knowledge of the truth, are converted unto the Lord, and honor and remember sacred covenants, then the promised blessing is that we never will fall away. We eagerly will set aside the weapons of rebellion in our lives. Our turn to the Lord and away from self will be "steadfast and immovable" (Mosiah

5:15). And our capacity to live more in alignment with what we know will be enlarged.

By divine design, discipleship is demanding. But only as we expend our moral agency to conform our lives to His will and timing—as we lose our life for His sake—can we ultimately find it (see Matthew 10:37–39).

The Role of a Teacher

As we turn resolutely to the Savior, we are blessed with "a love of God and *of all men*" (2 Nephi 31:20; emphasis added) and are drawn to serve our brothers and sisters. The natural consequence of coming unto Christ with real intent and striving to be perfected in Him (see Moroni 10:32) is turning outward in service and compassion. Thus, the selfishness of the natural man is replaced by the selflessness of a saint as we turn to the Lord and invite into our lives the rich blessings of His infinite and eternal Atonement.

Every person who enters into sacred covenants and becomes a member of The Church of Jesus Christ of Latter-day Saints is a teacher—at all times and in all places. Teaching is one of the most important types of service we can render in our homes and in the Church because helping others to learn and live gospel truths is eternally important and personally edifying.

We should always remember that the Holy Ghost is the ultimate and true teacher—not us. You and I as teachers have the responsibility to preach the gospel by the Spirit, even the Comforter, as a prerequisite for the learning by faith that is obtained only by and through the Holy Ghost (see Doctrine and Covenants 50:14). But the lessons we teach and the testimonies we bear are preparatory to a learner's acting and learning for himself or herself.

Regardless of how worthy we are and how effectively we teach, you and I simply cannot push or force truth into the hearts of learners. Teaching, exhorting, explaining, and testifying, as important as they are, can never convey or transfer to a learner a witness of the truthfulness of the restored gospel. Our best efforts can only bring the message of truth *unto* the heart (see 2 Nephi 33:1). Ultimately, a learner needs to act in righteousness and thereby invite the truth *into* his or her own heart. Only in this way can honest seekers of truth develop the spiritual capacity to find answers for themselves—and "to stand as witnesses of God at all times and in all things, and in all places" (Mosiah 18:9). As teachers, one of our most important responsibilities is to invite learners to act—to exercise their moral agency in accordance with the teachings of the Savior.

Teaching the gospel the Lord's way includes observing, listening, and discerning as prerequisites to talking. The sequence of these four interrelated processes is significant. Please note that active observing and listening precede discerning—and that observing, listening, and discerning come before speaking. Employing this pattern enables an instructor to identify and teach to the needs of learners.

As we observe, listen, and discern, we can be given "in the very hour that portion that shall be meted unto every man" (Doctrine and Covenants 84:85)—the truths to emphasize and the answers to give that will meet the specific needs of a particular individual or group. Only by observing, listening, and discerning can we be guided by the Spirit to say and do the things that will be most helpful to those whom we teach and serve. Parents and gospel instructors who talk without observing, listening, and discerning teach neither lessons nor people. Rather, they talk to themselves in front of learners.

As representatives of the Savior, you and I have the ongoing responsibility to work diligently and to implant in our hearts and minds the fundamental doctrines and principles of the restored gospel, especially from the Book of Mormon. As we do so, the promised blessing is that the Holy Ghost will "bring all things to [our] remembrance" (John 14:26) and empower us as we teach and testify. But, the Spirit can only work with and through us if we give Him something with which to work. He cannot help us remember things we have not labored to learn.

Effective service as a teacher requires personal worthiness, humility, continual treasuring up of the words of life, discernment, and an understanding of who we are as representatives of Jesus Christ. As we thus prepare ourselves for this sacred service, we become instruments in the hands of God to assist His children in finding answers to the questions of the soul—answers always contained in the fulness of the restored gospel of Jesus Christ.

Power to Become: Spiritual Patterns for Pressing Forward with a Steadfastness in Christ

As we honor sacred covenants, obey God's commandments, seek for the companionship of the Holy Ghost, and fulfill faithfully our personal responsibilities to "increase in learning" (Proverbs 9:9) and "act in doctrine" (Doctrine and Covenants 101:78), we can be blessed with the "power to become."

The primary outcomes of devoted discipleship are to "awaken" unto God (see Alma 5:7; 7:22), to be "born again" (John 3:3; Mosiah 27:25; Alma 5:49; 7:14), to put off the natural man (see Mosiah 3:19), and to become "new" in Christ. "Therefore if any man be in Christ, he is a new creature: old things are passed away; behold, all things are become new" (2 Corinthians 5:17). We also are to press forward with steadfastness in Christ (see 2 Nephi 31:20) and endure in faith on His name to the end (see Matthew 24:13; 2 Nephi 31:16; Doctrine and Covenants 14:7; 20:29).

Ultimately, followers of Christ are to become like Him.

In the Strength of the Lord

Righteous learning and acting can lead to "becoming" only by and through and because of the Savior's Atonement. The word *become* denotes growing, developing, changing, transforming, and converting. As we "come unto Christ" and seek perfection in and through Him (see Moroni 10:32–33), we incrementally and increasingly obtain His mind (see Philippians 2:5) and character. We put off the natural man and are fundamentally changed, transformed, and "converted unto the Lord" (Alma 23:6). Heavenly Father's plan of happiness establishes the framework for eternal progression, and the gospel of Jesus Christ provides the doctrines, covenants, and ordinances necessary to become what children of God are intended to become.

The absolute enormity of perfection as an eternal goal or outcome may cause us to feel helplessly overwhelmed, inadequate, and discouraged. But perfection is not achieved all at once or in mortality. Even our perfect example, the Savior, progressed "line upon line, precept upon precept" (2 Nephi 28:30).

We also do not pursue perfection alone or relying exclusively upon the puny possibilities of the natural man or woman in each of us. We can depend upon help, strength, and support from heaven.

For disciples of Jesus Christ, the journey of mortality proceeds along the pathway to perfection. The Savior's Atonement strengthens and enables us to press forward with steadfastness and perseverance. Our limited mortal capacity can be enlarged to meet the requirements of the divine injunction—"Be ye therefore perfect" (Matthew 5:48).

As we increase in learning about the attributes and character of the Savior and act in His doctrine, we are blessed with the power to become. We receive grace for grace and are strengthened to do good and to become better through the infinite and eternal Atonement. Our direction on the pathway of perfection becomes increasingly clear and our pace ever more steady. We are blessed to "press forward with a steadfastness in Christ, having a perfect brightness of hope, and a love of God and of all men. Wherefore, if ye shall press forward, feasting upon the word of Christ, and endure to the end, behold, thus saith the Father: Ye shall have eternal life.

"And now, behold, my beloved brethren, this is the way; and there is none other way nor name given under heaven whereby man can be saved in the kingdom of God. And now, behold, this is the doctrine of Christ, and the only and true doctrine of the Father, and of the Son, and of the Holy Ghost, which is one God, without end. Amen" (2 Nephi 31:20–21).

The Spiritual Gift of Personal Peace

As we endeavor to live righteously and pursue perfection appropriately, we can receive through the Atonement enlarged capacity, spiritual gifts, and supernal blessings. One of the greatest spiritual gifts we can be given as we press forward along the strait and narrow path is personal peace. The spiritual gift of personal peace is the foundation upon which the power to become is established.

We often encounter obstacles of various kinds and unanticipated delays as we progress along the pathway to perfection in the journey of mortality. However, personal peace provides a perspective, a settledness, and a tranquillity that help us to keep our focus fixed on our eternal destination—in spite of life's challenges and disappointments.

The world searches to and fro for peace and often believes personal fulfillment is to be found in material possessions, in prestige and prominence, or in the interpersonal advice so readily dispensed in the self-help section of a local bookstore. Such approaches to finding peace wholly and totally miss the mark—which is the Lord Jesus Christ.

Peace originates in Christ and comes from and because of Him. And it is imperative that we remember—it is His peace that He gives unto us.

Faith in the Lord Jesus Christ—that is, total trust in Him, complete confidence in Him, and a ready reliance on His merits, mercy, and grace—leads to hope. Because of the Savior's Atonement, that hope in the power of the Resurrection and in eternal life invites the sweet peace of conscience for which men and women have always yearned. The redeeming and cleansing power of the Savior's Atonement helps us to dispel the despair caused by transgression and sin. And the enabling and strengthening aspect of the Atonement helps us to see and to do and to become good in ways that we could never recognize or accomplish with our limited mortal capacity.

Our understanding of the plan of happiness and of the role of the infinite and eternal Atonement allows us to see somewhat beyond the boundaries and limitations of mortality. And when we are then confronted with the greatest challenges of our mortal existence, a loving Savior grants unto us a peace that extends beyond mortality and into eternity—a peace of conscience that cannot be comprehended in earthly or rational terms.

The personal peace that comes into our lives through faith in the Lord Jesus Christ can strengthen us to face, overcome, and learn from adversity. Every human soul yearns for peace—even peace of conscience and the peace that passeth all understanding. This blessing is not obtained with worldly wealth or through professional accomplishment, personal prominence, prestige, or power. The Lord Jesus Christ is the only source of enduring, personal peace. Faith and hope in Him, obedience to His commandments, and pressing forward valiantly along the path of perfection invite the spiritual gift of peace into our lives. And His peace fortifies us to face adversity with assurance and perspective.

Priesthood Ordinances and Willing Obedience

For mortal men and women, the power to become is possible because of and through the Atonement of Jesus Christ. "We believe that through the Atonement of Christ, all mankind may be saved, by obedience to the laws and ordinances of the Gospel" (Articles of Faith 1:3).

Priesthood ordinances and willing obedience are essential as we press forward along the pathway to perfection in the journey of mortality.

Ordinances performed by proper priesthood authority and received worthily provide access to all of the blessings made possible through the Savior's atoning sacrifice. Without the blessings and gifts of the Atonement received through priesthood ordinances, our progress in mortality and eternity would be thwarted.

An ordinance is a sacred, formal act performed by the authority of the priesthood that helps us learn and remember who we are as children of God; it also reminds us of our spiritual responsibilities and duties. The Lord has provided ordinances to help us come unto Him and receive eternal life. As we honor ordinances, He strengthens us.

Priesthood ordinances open the door and provide access to the power of godliness. To come unto the Savior, an individual *must* first pass through the gate of baptism and receive the gift of the Holy Ghost—and then continue to press forward along the path of covenants and ordinances that leads to the Savior and the blessings of His Atonement (see 2 Nephi 31). Priesthood ordinances are essential to fully "come unto Christ, and be perfected in him" (Moroni 10:32; see also vv. 30–33). Without the ordinances, an individual cannot receive all of the blessings made possible through the Lord's infinite and eternal atoning sacrifice (see Alma 34:10–14)—even the power of godliness.

The first law of heaven is obedience—the aligning of our individual will with God's will. Obedience operates at a number of different levels and is not simply a passive, steady state. Rather, obedience grows and develops and deepens and increases and expands. Our experience with and understanding of the principle of obedience should change as we develop spiritually and as we gain additional light and knowledge—line upon line and precept upon precept. Also, our spiritual expectations should increase and intensify as we continue to faithfully obey God's commandments.

Closely associated with obeying with a willing heart is reaching a point where we no longer are driven or directed by *rules;* instead, we learn to govern our lives by *principle.* To be sure, we keep the rules, but we also begin to ask ourselves, "What is the principle involved here?" Such a person becomes less dependent upon external scaffolding and structure and more dependent upon quiet and ongoing divine direction. As the Prophet Joseph explained, "I teach them correct principles, and they govern themselves" (*The Teachings of Joseph Smith*, 32).

The pathway to perfection in our mortal journey takes us to and through "letter of the law" obedience to public and institutional commandments and toward the spirit of devoted discipleship and a private, personal, and individual change of heart.

Obedience to gospel principles and ordinances frees a person from the spiritual bondage of sin (see John 8:31–36). As we obtain a desire and determination to obey God's commandments with all of our hearts and with willing minds, we can qualify for and be blessed to receive "commandments not a few" and "revelations in their time" (Doctrine and Covenants 59:4). Such personal and private direction from our loving Heavenly Father is a supernal source of assurance, enlightenment, and joy.

Enduring Valiantly

In mortality we chart our course and begin to become what we ultimately will be in eternity. Our second estate (see Abraham 3:26) is not a probationary experience to be tolerated reluctantly and grudgingly. Rather, the scriptures indicate that we are to "*press forward* with a steadfastness in Christ, having a perfect brightness of hope, and a love of God and of all men. Wherefore, if ye shall press forward, feasting upon the word of Christ, and *endure to the end,* behold, thus saith the Father: Ye shall have eternal life" (2 Nephi 31:20; emphasis added).

"All thrones and dominions, principalities and powers, shall be revealed and set forth upon all who have *endured valiantly* for the gospel of Jesus Christ" (Doctrine and Covenants 121:29; emphasis added).

Vital spiritual patterns are evident in the life of the Savior, in the scriptures, and in the teachings of living prophets and apostles. These spiritual patterns are now and always have been important aids to discernment and sources of direction and protection for faithful Latter-day Saints. And spiritual patterns are essential in avoiding the deception that is so pervasive in our world today.

A powerful pattern the Lord uses to advance His work and to tutor Heavenly Father's children upon the earth is "small and simple things."

"Behold I say unto you, that by small and simple things are great things brought to pass; and small means in many instances doth confound the wise" (Alma 37:6).

"Wherefore, be not weary in well-doing, for ye are laying the foundation of a great work. And out of small things proceedeth that which is great" (Doctrine and Covenants 64:33).

This pattern is especially relevant for faithful disciples of the Savior who are striving to endure valiantly to the end.

The spiritual pattern of small and simple things bringing forth great things produces firmness and steadfastness, deepening devotion, and more complete conversion to the Lord Jesus Christ and His gospel. As you and I become increasingly steadfast and immovable, we are less prone to zealous and exaggerated spurts of spirituality followed by extended periods of slackness. A spiritual "spurter" is one who is given to short bursts of spectacular effort followed by frequent and lengthy periods of rest.

We can avoid or overcome unsustainable spiritual spurting as we employ the Lord's pattern of small and simple things and become valiant disciples with strong, spiritual stamina—blessed with capacity to endure to the end with faith in the Savior.

Knowing and understanding our divine identity as children of a loving Heavenly Father should influence everything about and relating to us—what we think, what we do, where we go, what we eat, what we drink, what we wear, and a multitude of other decisions and actions. This fundamental truth is central to enduring to the end valiantly and becoming all that the Father and the Son yearn for us to become.

As we strive to endure valiantly to the end, the lessons that can be learned from repeated study of the war chapters in the Book of Mormon have great value and applicability for us. A number of episodes in this sacred volume of scripture highlight the truth that accurate awareness of an enemy's intent leads to appropriate preparations for battle.

The intent of our enemy in the latter-day war in which we are engaged is quite clear. The Father's plan is designed to provide direction for His children, to help them become happy, and to bring them safely home to Him with resurrected, exalted bodies. Heavenly Father desires us to be together in the light and filled with hope. In contrast, Lucifer labors to make the sons and daughters of God confused and unhappy and to hinder their eternal progression. The overarching intent of the father of lies is that all of us would become "miserable like unto himself" (2 Nephi 2:27). Lucifer wants us ultimately to be alone in the dark and without hope.

As we learn and understand who we are as sons and daughters of God, and as we are blessed with discernment about the intent of our enemies, we can be blessed to endure valiantly and well. Challenges and trials will not be eliminated from our lives, but through the Atonement of Jesus Christ our spiritual strength and capacity will be increased and enlarged.

ACCEPTED OF THE LORD

We learn in the *Lectures on Faith* that three basic things are "necessary in order that any rational and intelligent being may exercise faith in [the Father and the Son] unto life and salvation:" (1) the idea that They actually exist, (2) a correct idea of Their character, perfections, and attributes, and (3) "an actual knowledge that the course of life which he [or she] is pursuing is according to [God's] will" (*Lectures on Faith,* 38). Please note that the sinless and selfless nature of the Savior's character and perfections, the blessings available in our lives through the infinite and eternal atoning sacrifice, and the possibilities and pitfalls of our mortal pathway to perfection have been emphasized repeatedly in *Increase in Learning, Act in Doctrine,* and *Power to Become.* Each of these three major themes is related to the requirements for the exercise of true faith in God.

Consider the responsibility each of us has as a disciple to obtain an actual knowledge that the course of life we are pursuing is according to God's will. Can such knowledge be obtained in mortality? Can I truly come to know that the path I am pursuing in my life pleases God? And if it is possible to know these things, how can I know? Such questions indeed are some of the most pointed and poignant questions of the soul.

As we increase in learning about the Savior and His gospel, as we strive with ever greater consistency to act in His doctrine, ordinances, and covenants, then we are blessed with power through His Atonement to increasingly become like Him. Our hearts and natures are changed, and our desires are directed to Him and His purposes. His will supersedes our will. Such changes rarely occur quickly, dramatically, or all at once; rather, they come into our lives "line upon line, precept upon precept, here a little and there a little" (2 Nephi 28:30).

But how can we really know how we are doing, and if our course is in accordance with God's will?

Simple but powerful indicators of our progress have been posted along the pathway to perfection—road signs that provide timely

1. Am I incrementally and steadily *increasing in learning* about the things of eternity that matter most, such as the nature of the Godhead, the plan of salvation, the reality and divinity of the Lord Jesus Christ, the efficacy of the Savior's infinite and eternal atoning sacrifice, and the Restoration of the gospel in the latter days? Is my capacity expanding to obtain answers to important spiritual questions through diligent study and the power of the Holy Ghost?

2. Is what I am learning incrementally and steadily reflected in how I *act in the doctrine* of Christ? Can I detect progress in reducing the disparity between what I know about the gospel and how I live the gospel? Am I turning from self to the Savior?

3. Is what I am learning and how I am acting in the doctrine enabling me to incrementally and steadily receive the *power to become* what God yearns for me to become? Am I pressing forward on the pathway to perfection?

information about our direction and pace. A few questions can help sharpen our focus on the information contained on those signs.

If we can answer yes to these questions, or at least acknowledge progress moving in the right direction in spite of some weaving from side to side on the strait and narrow path, periodic stops and starts, and unintended detours, then indeed we can know the course in life we are pursuing is in accordance with God's will. Our results may not be flashy or appear outwardly impressive to other people. And we certainly have not arrived at our ultimate and final destination. But steadiness in accomplishing these basic gospel imperatives of learning, acting, and becoming is an important part of God's desire for each of His children.

"An actual knowledge to any person, that the course of life which he pursues is according to the will of God, is essentially necessary to enable him to have that confidence in God without which no person can obtain eternal life" (*Lectures on Faith,* 67).

"Such was, and always will be, the situation of the saints of God, that unless they have an actual knowledge that the course they are pursuing is according to the will of God they will grow weary in their minds, and faint" (*Lectures on Faith,* 67–68).

"Let us here observe, that a religion that does not require the sacrifice of all things never has power sufficient to produce the faith necessary unto life and salvation; for, from the first existence of man, the faith necessary unto the enjoyment of life and salvation never could be obtained without the sacrifice of all earthly things. It was through this sacrifice, and this only, that God has ordained that men should enjoy eternal life; and it is through the medium of the sacrifice of all earthly things that men do actually know that they are doing the things that are well pleasing in the sight of God" (*Lectures on Faith,* 69).

"But those who have not made this sacrifice to God do not know that the course which they pursue is well pleasing in his sight; for whatever may be their belief or their opinion, it is a matter of doubt and uncertainty in their mind; and where doubt and uncertainty are there faith is not, nor can it be. For doubt and faith do not exist in the same person at the same time; so that persons whose minds are under doubts and fears cannot have unshaken confidence; and where unshaken confidence is not there faith is weak; and where faith is weak the persons will not be able to contend against all the opposition, tribulations, and afflictions which they will have to encounter in order to be heirs of God, and joint-heirs with Christ Jesus; and they will grow weary in their minds, and the adversary will have power over them and destroy them" (*Lectures on Faith*, 71).

As the Saints in Missouri were subjected to severe persecution in 1833 and forced to sign an agreement to leave Jackson County, the following revelation was given to the Prophet Joseph Smith:

"Verily I say unto you, all among them who know their hearts are honest, and are broken, and their spirits contrite, and are willing to observe their covenants by sacrifice—yea, every sacrifice which I, the Lord, shall command—*they are accepted of me.*

"For I, the Lord, will cause them to bring forth as a very fruitful tree which is planted in a goodly land, by a pure stream, that yieldeth much precious fruit" (Doctrine and Covenants 97:8–9; emphasis added).

Each of us can invite the Holy Ghost to help us assess "things as they really are" (Jacob 4:13) about our progress along the pathway of covenants, obedience, and service. He will teach us plainly and directly about the honesty of our hearts, about the contrite nature of our spirits, and about our willingness to observe our covenants by sacrifice, even every sacrifice which the Lord shall command. Being accepted of the Lord certainly is a key element in the affirmation that the course we are pursuing in this life is in accordance with God's holy mind and will. And such assurance can be received as we press forward in our mortal journey on the pathway to perfection.

Nephi was a faithful and diligent son of Helaman. His public reign and sacred ministry among the Nephites and Lamanites spanned nearly forty years, ending just before the birth of the Savior. A scriptural description of Nephi provides important principles for us today.

"And it came to pass that there arose a division among the people, insomuch that they divided hither and thither and went their ways, leaving Nephi alone, as he was standing in the midst of them.

"And it came to pass that Nephi went his way towards his own house, *pondering upon the things which the Lord had shown unto him.*

"And it came to pass *as he was thus pondering*—being much cast down because of the wickedness of the people of the Nephites, their secret works of darkness, and their murderings, and their plunderings, and all manner of iniquities—and it came to pass *as he was thus pondering in his heart,* behold, a voice came unto him saying:

"Blessed art thou, Nephi, for those things which thou hast done; for I have beheld how thou hast with *unwearyingness* declared the word, which I have given unto thee, unto this people. And thou hast not feared them, and hast not sought thine own life, but hast sought my will, and to keep my commandments.

"And now, because thou hast done this with such *unwearyingness,* behold, I will bless thee forever; and I will make thee mighty in word and in deed, in faith and in works; yea, even that all things shall be done unto thee according to thy word, for thou shalt not ask that which is contrary to my will.

"Behold, thou art Nephi, and I am God. Behold, I declare it unto thee in the presence of mine angels, that *ye shall have power*" (Helaman 10:1–6; emphasis added).

Nephi learned, understood, and performed his duty with un-wearyingness. Facing opposition and difficulty, he pondered the things the Lord had shown him, was steadfast in turning from self to the Savior, and sought only to do God's will.

Each of us as a disciple of Christ can likewise ponder on the things the Lord has shown unto and done for us, and we can learn and act in our individual lives with unwearyingness. We will not receive precisely the same blessings that were bestowed upon Nephi, but we will be blessed with power—even the power to become.

"Learn of me, and listen to my words; walk in the meek-ness of my Spirit, and you shall have peace in me" (Doctrine and Covenants 19:23).

"Behold, I am Jesus Christ, the Son of God. I am the life and the light of the world.

"I am the same who came unto mine own and mine own re-ceived me not;

"But verily, verily, I say unto you, that as many as receive me, to them will I give *power to become* the sons of God, even to them that believe on my name. Amen" (Doctrine and Covenants 11:28–30; emphasis added).

Related Readings

1. Dieter F. Uchtdorf, "A Matter of a Few Degrees," *Ensign,* May 2008, 57–60.

2. Thomas S. Monson, "Decisions Determine Destiny," CES Fireside, November 6, 2005. Available online at speeches.byu. edu.

3. Gordon B. Hinckley, "This Is the Work of the Master," *Ensign,* May 1995, 69–71.

4. Ezra Taft Benson, "The Book of Mormon—Keystone of Our Religion," *Ensign,* November 1986, 4–7.

5. Bruce R. McConkie, "The Caravan Moves On," *Ensign,* November 1984, 82–85.

6. LeGrand Richards, "One Lord, One Faith, One Baptism," *Ensign,* May 1975, 95–97.

7. LeGrand Richards, "I Am More Interested in the Long Hereafter," BYU Devotional, February 25, 1975. Available online at speeches.byu.edu.

8. Spencer W. Kimball, "Planning for a Full and Abundant Life," *Ensign,* May 1974, 86–89.

9. Boyd K. Packer, "The Only True and Living Church," *Ensign,* December 1971, 40–42.

10. Spencer W. Kimball, "Tragedy or Destiny?" BYU Devotional, December 6, 1955. Available (audio only) at speeches .byu.edu. Also available in print as "Tragedy or Destiny?" chapter 2 in *Teachings of Presidents of the Church: Spencer W. Kimball* (2006), 11–21.

Explore these concepts further with a group discussion.

Scan this code or visit
seek.deseretbook.com/powertobecome

CONSIDER

What am I learning about the importance of righteous patterns in learning, acting, and becoming?

CONSIDER

How can I apply more effectively in my gospel learning and living the principle of "all things gathered together in one"?

CONSIDER

What am I learning about observing my covenants by sacrifice and being accepted of the Lord?

My Own Questions to Consider

SCRIPTURES RELATED TO WHAT I AM LEARNING

AN INVITATION TO LEARN, TO ACT, AND TO BECOME		
What additional doctrines and principles, if understood, would help me to continue pressing forward with steadfastness on the pathway to perfection?	What can and should I do to act in those doctrines and principles?	How will I know if I am making progress in striving to become more like the Savior?

AN INVITATION TO LEARN, TO ACT, AND TO BECOME		
What additional doctrines and principles, if understood, would help me to continue pressing forward with steadfastness on the pathway to perfection?	What can and should I do to act in those doctrines and principles?	How will I know if I am making progress in striving to become more like the Savior?

AN INVITATION TO LEARN, TO ACT, AND TO BECOME		
What additional doctrines and principles, if understood, would help me to continue pressing forward with steadfastness on the pathway to perfection?	What can and should I do to act in those doctrines and principles?	How will I know if I am making progress in striving to become more like the Savior?

Sources Cited

Bell, James P. *In the Strength of the Lord: The Life and Teachings of James E. Faust.* 1999.

Benson, Ezra Taft. *God, Family, Country: Our Three Great Loyalties.* 1974.

———."A New Witness for Christ." *Ensign,* November 1984, 6–8.

"The Family: A Proclamation to the World." *Ensign,* November 2010, 129.

Hafen, Bruce C. *A Disciple's Life: The Biography of Neal A. Maxwell.* 2002.

Hinckley, Gordon B. "A Principle with a Promise." *Improvement Era,* 1965, 521.

Holland, Jeffrey R. "'The Peaceable Things of the Kingdom.'" *Ensign,* November 1996, 82–84.

Hymns of The Church of Jesus Christ of Latter-day Saints. 1985.

Jones, Daniel W. *Forty Years among the Indians.*1890.

Kimball, Spencer W. *Faith Precedes the Miracle.* 1972.

———. *The Teachings of Spencer W. Kimball.* Edited by Edward L. Kimball. 1982.

Lectures on Faith. 1985.

Lee, Harold B. *Decisions for Successful Living.* 1973.

Liebman, Joshua Loth. *Peace of Mind.* 1946.

Maxwell, Neal A. "'Apply the Atoning Blood of Christ.'" *Ensign,* November 1997, 22–24.

———. *If Thou Endure It Well.* 1996.

———. "'Swallowed Up in the Will of the Father.'" *Ensign,* November 1995, 22–24.

———. *Wherefore, Ye Must Press Forward.* 1977.

McConkie, Bruce R. *Mormon Doctrine.* 2nd ed. rev. 1966.

Monson, Thomas S. "Obedience Brings Blessings." *Ensign,* May 2013, 89–92.

Nelson, Russell M. "A New Harvest Time." *Ensign,* May 1998, 34–36.

———. "Perfection Pending." *Ensign,* November 1995, 86–88.

Oaks, Dallin H. "The Challenge to Become." *Ensign,* November 2000, 32–34.

Packer, Boyd K. "Covenants." *Ensign,* May 1987, 22–25.

———. "Our Moral Environment." *Ensign,* May 1992, 66–68.

Preach My Gospel: A Guide to Missionary Service. 2004.

Smith, Joseph. *History of The Church of Jesus Christ of Latter-day Saints.* 7 vols. 1932–51.

———. *The Teachings of Joseph Smith.* Edited by Larry E. Dahl and Donald Q. Cannon. 1997.

Smith, Joseph Fielding. *Doctrines of Salvation.* 3 vols. Edited by Bruce R. McConkie. 1954–56.

Staheli, Donald L. "Obedience—Life's Great Challenge." *Ensign,* May 1998, 81–82.

Teachings of Presidents of the Church: David O. McKay. 2003.

Teachings of Presidents of the Church: George Albert Smith. 2011.

Teachings of Presidents of the Church: Heber J. Grant. 2002.

Teachings of Presidents of the Church: Joseph Smith. 2007.

Young, Brigham. *Discourses of Brigham Young.* Compiled by John A. Widtsoe. 1954.

INDEX

189

and, 88–89; conversion and, 159–60

Character: of Jesus Christ, 11–13, 155–57; David O. McKay on, 98

Charity, 2

Children, teaching obedience to, 95–97

Children of God, 122–31, 170–71

Church of Jesus Christ of Latter-day Saints, The: as living church, 152; teaching in, 161. *See also* Gospel

"Come, Come, Ye Saints," 26

Commandment(s): to be perfect, 5–11; personal, 87, 90–94, 169. *See also* Obedience

Compassion, 11, 156–57

Confirmation, 77

Conversion, 3, 159–61, 170

Covenants, 25, 77–80, 158

Crucifixion, 129–30

Dead, ordinances for, 78–83

Death, life after, 40–42, 43–44

Discernment: of enemy's intent, 131–37, 171; in teaching, 162

Discipleship: purposes of, 1–2; peace in, 38; armor in, 132–33; responsibilities of, 148, 149–50, 172; outcomes of, 163–64

Dispensation, final, 82–83

Divine identity, understanding, 122–31, 170–71

Doctrine: in framework for gospel learning, 153–55; acting in, 155, 173

Doubt, 174–75

Elijah, spirit of, 81–82

Enduring: salvation through, 108–10; importance of, 110–11; patterns in, 111–21, 137–38, 169–70; and understanding divine identity, 122–31, 170–71; and discerning intent of adversary, 131–37, 171. *See also* Pressing forward

Enemy, discerning intent of, 131–37, 171

Faith: peace through, 46–47, 166; to be healed or not healed, 54–62; exercising, in God and Jesus Christ, 171–72; through sacrifice, 174; doubt and, 174–75

Family: peace from knowledge of eternal, 40–42; genealogical work and, 78–79. *See also* Home

"Family: A Proclamation to the World, The," 122–23

Fast offerings, 90

Faust, James E., 78

Fear: faith and, 59–60, 174–75; of blessing sacrament, 115–16; preparation and, 133

Final dispensation, 82–83

Final Judgment, 3

Frehner, Albert, 90–92

Frehner, Matilda Reber, 90–92

Fulness of times, dispensation of, 82–83

Genealogy, 78–79

God: becoming like, 4, 8; children of, 122–31, 170–71; covenanting with, 158; exercising faith in, 171–72. *See also* Will of God